ROW:53 SEATS:DE&F

THE TRUTH
BEHIND
DEPORTATION

1982 - 2000

Parliamentary Licence
P2006000398

BARRY SOUTHON

This book has been printed digitally and produced in a standard specification in order to ensure its continuing availability

Published by
Antony Rowe Publishing Services in 2007
48-50 Birch Close
Eastbourne
East Sussex
BN23 6PE
England

ISBN (10) 1905200625
ISBN (13) 9781905200627

Printed and bound by CPI Antony Rowe, Eastbourne

Malcolm K Southon

Thomas Johnson

Ian Loudon

Cynthia Halls

Throughout the voyage of life
we all encounter many people.
Some are special
a few are even exceptional.

Our lives are
enhanced by such encounters.

INTRODUCTION

We are ordinary individuals who have been involved in the deportation to most countries throughout the world of classified "High Risk" subjects from 1982 through until 2000. I can speak with some authority of the Home Office modus operandi...

...warts and all!

This subject invokes diverse opinions and often comments based on totally incorrect or frequently questionable information. Deportation is a highly emotive subject which needs to be addressed in an apolitical and unprejudiced way.

I feel motivated to set out a view from inside the channels of deportation precisely what occurs at the front end. The view may not be popular or Politically Correct but it's the truth and we insiders bear the scars to prove it.

It was my pleasure to work with a great team of people whom I was proud to call colleagues and friends.

Without exception, each member of the team contributed a wealth of experience and complete commitment to the task.

Often dealing with difficult high-risk individuals, under extremely testing circumstances. Frequently encountering obstructive violent behaviour, which manifested itself in various forms. Being bitten, spat at, kicked, verbally abused, punched or slashed with a razor, even faeces thrown at you. We all sampled such abuse, and then came back for more and yet more.

Obstructive and abusive behaviour did not always emanate from the subject being removed. A few Immigration officers were not beyond throwing a tantrum either.

One or two airline personnel could also be obstructive in the extreme. Even when the airline was directly responsible for the subject's arrival in the UK through poor pre-check in scrutiny or questionable documentation.

Effectually the authority (HM Immigration) was regularly given the finger by some airlines.

Enforcement Legislation existed but was not invoked.

WHERE WE ARE FROM: THE FORMATIVE YEARS.

SEPTEMBER 1943 my mother along with other pregnant women from South East London was moved to rural areas in order to safely give birth in relative tranquil conditions compared to the London blitz.

I was born on a cold winter's day in October 1943 at Chippinghurst Manor, Denton, Oxford. Alas, that was as close as I ever came to the Manor Born and the cloisters of Oxford.

Returning to south-east London my parents were, along with many others, making do the best that they could, in war-time London.

The family on my father's side can be traced back to the Huguenot lace-maker's arrival in Bethnal Green east London from France some three hundred years ago.

My father was in the Royal Artillery and my Mother was making a home as best she could.

The Blitz took it's toll and we, along with thousands of others, were bombed out three times in total throughout the duration of the war, my parents losing all of their gathered possessions each time...a mere inconvenience. At least we survived. The closest near miss was a shopping trip to Woolworth's at New Cross. A V1 rocket scored a direct hit. The casualty list was heavy and the store was demolished. My mother and I survived more by luck than judgement.

Having lost our homes, (flats in Musgrove Road, Shardloes Road and Omney Road) we finished up living in a nissen hut located at 116B Jerningham Road, which stood at the top of a steep tree-lined hill. From the top of the hill we had extensive views over south London towards Greenwich, the Thames, and beyond.

Our nissen hut was one of ten located on a cleared bomb-site. The building was basic, a concrete floor, rooms divided by hardboard, a semi-circular shaped corrugated roof, made of asbestos. Dampness was a major problem but it was home. The outside toilet was next to the coal-shed. Our bath was a tin, four feet long, shaped container placed in front of the fire and half filled once a week, on Fridays as I remember, from boiled kettles. We all shared the water. Other days it was a wash down in the large sink. One functioning cold tap provided water. Hot water came from the kettle on the hob.

My first brother, Malcolm, joined us in April 1946. Our father at this time cycled from Deptford to Acton and back each day for his work as a surgical instrument maker. Whilst our mother worked each evening at Peak Freans biscuit factory in Bermondsey. Broken biscuits and miss-shaped Newbury fruits were an occasional bonus of her toil.

During this period, I became an astronaut at the age of six. My father acquired a Triumph motor-cycle which had a side-car attached to it. For some reason, the side-car was detached and remained in the garden, providing a great opportunity for endless hours of play. I used the side-car as either a rocket or a Spitfire cockpit by forming a circle with thumb and forefinger of each hand, and by placing our fingers to our eyes, the goggles were in place. We took off. With Malcolm sitting in the back of the side-car and the hinged roof lowered, we were airborne. Moon and back by tea time in the rocket. Or reliving the battle of Britain in our Spitfire cockpit which served in many imaginary conflicts, which we survived unscathed. The more we played the greater fun it was.

Baked beans on toast interrupted many an adventure. Being hauled in doors having failed to respond to my mother's repeated calls often concluded such adventures of the time. What did she expect? We were in another world. It smelt musty and was falling apart but could it fly and fuel consumption was fantastic. In fact I'm not sure I understood that fuel was used to propel a rocket.

Primary schooling commenced at St James, Hatcham. The head master William (Bill) Goodchild ruled with an iron fist. I encountered his wrath on five occasions, being caned five times in front of the assembled school. Six strokes of the bamboo cane, three delivered with force on each palm of the hand, me biting my lip to avoid crying in front of my peers. I soon became hardened to the pain and maybe even anti-authority to some extent. Why did he always seem to pick on me? That was a frequent question in my mind. To this day, I still feel I never deserved the severity of that level of punishment. My misdemeanours were minor; talking in class or flicking a paper pellet or just getting caught not paying attention. I was a slow learner and it wasn't until the sixth time I was sent to the head master's office that it dawned on me, if you don't knock he doesn't cane you. After a short while, I returned to my class and told the teacher that the head master was out. I got away with the lie. I was not caned again.

Life consisted of primary education, taking care of my brother and helping the milkman who delivered to us. He drove a Co-op milk-cart pulled by a shire horse the like of which I had never seen before. As I mentioned previously Jerningham Road was steep and a long haul for those living at the top. The milkman would steer the laden cart in a series of S shaped manoeuvres in order to retain control of the heavy weight and make the task easier on the horse. I would jump off the cart and deliver the bottles of milk as dictated by the milkman.

The Shire horse would wend its way up the hill farting and dumping huge piles of manure in its wake. As the journey unfolded, people in the neighbourhood would appear with buckets and a shovel in hand. The manure would disappear almost as fast as it appeared. These efforts produced the finest rhubarb and roses in the area; I'm in no doubt. I would not be surprised if every movement was strategically monitored from the window of interested parties as we progressed up the hill. Manure retrieval was of high importance to those involved in home- grown food production.

1949 produced yet another brother, Derek, in November. I recall Malcolm and me sitting on a chair as our mother brought Derek home from the Hospital. We were allowed to hold him. He slept in a drawer which had been removed from a cupboard until he outgrew it. A factor that figured in all of our early days was sleeping in that drawer; it saved buying a cot. Malcolm and I slept in the same bed, one each end, feet kicking in the middle: the source of many disturbances.

No television, just a radio and the benefit of a fertile imagination, which resulted in our flights to the moon long, before the Americans. An uncle gave me my first bike, of which I was very proud. It was a heavy sit-up-and-beg-type with a fixed wheel; it was far too big for me, I couldn't sit on the saddle and reach the pedals at the same time. So I rode it in a half on, unseated position, balancing on the pedals. This aspect took some getting used to, and resulted in me going over the handlebars on numerous occasions. It was a very painful   learning curve but I was determined to master the art of riding a bike. I was under strict instructions not to ride on the roads and forbidden to leave the neighbourhood. Sure: I conformed for a while, and then kind of stretched the limits; I needed to explore further field. I was eight years old-how much more growing did I need to do?

I would regularly take myself off on the bike to Surrey Docks. I'd position myself alongside the swing bridge prior to the lock entrance to the River Thames. By standing on the cycle, I was just able to see over the steel bridge construction. As ships passed, and I would yell out at the top of my voice "Where you going Mr?" Eager to hear the reply, Africa, India, Sweden, America would be bellowed back more often than not. A deep fascination for ships developed together with a longing to see what was beyond Deptford and Bermondsey. There just had to be more out in the rest of the world and I needed to see it.

Telegraph Hill was our nearest park and green field area: a venue for us to unleash our energy as growing lads; football played with a heavy leather, often water-soaked, ball. We walked everywhere when we were out together so exercise was never lacking. Greenwich Park and Blackheath were further away. Both were regular destinations for Sunday walks, with the added treat of watching people sailing their boats on the ponds, or playing in football matches at weekends during the winter. I recall another attraction on the walks was the fact that we passed "Nobles" a large imposing toy and sports shop at Deptford Bridge. A vast window display would hold me spell-bound for ages. Many times I was dragged away by the ear having failed to respond to calls.

These walks always included spelling tests for Malcolm and me. We were called upon to read signs and hoardings regardless of details on advertisement. Persistence ruled. You got it right before we moved on. Some walks took an eternity. As a five year old, Dunlop always gave me difficulty because lettered vertically on a huge chimney just off of Greenwich High Road behind the Miller Hospital.

Times were hard and money was scarce, hand-me-downs provided the clothing. Mum did her best and we never worried or went hungry. We survived and enjoyed life as it came. Don't get the wrong impression: I'm not whingeing; I'm just trying to set the scene.

Our nearest relatives lived on the outskirts of Sidcup and Welling in Kent (the real country as far as we knew) whilst other parts of the family were located in the opposite direction across the river in Leytonstone, east London. Our visits to Wanstead flats seemed like the country to us as kids then. Kite flying was a firm favourite. I had an ex- RAF yellow box-kite of which I was extremely proud; we would fly the kite every chance we had. Visits at Christmas or family occasions were a big treat. A train journey plus a long walk resulted in lots of fun sharing our cousin's toys and watching their television. A whole different world from what we knew.

One incident I'll never forget and neither has Derek. For some reason we were in a Lyons tea shop which was located near to New Cross. Whilst Malcolm and I were seated, Derek sitting in his pushchair, mum was at the counter. On the table were salt and pepper and a tub of mustard with a spoon in it. I had no idea what it was. I scooped up a large spoonful and gave it to Derek; that's what you did, feed your brother. The screams were supersonic. Derek has never had a liking for mustard since that day. I won't relate what happened next... other than to say I also had a very hot spot too.

EDUCATION

MY FORMAL EDUCATION was lacking to some degree, not that I failed to make the effort. I did try, but I seemed always to be the strongest and supported the rest from the bottom of the class. Classes consisted of thirty-five to forty children. The teachers, task was not that easy either, I have no doubt they did the best they could with the resources available.

All of my term reports clearly stated "needs to try harder, more effort required". I obtained basic certificates of education, basic is not an overstatement. I can't recall any teaching experience which ignited any enthusiasm in me, or which sparked my basic interest. Constant rebuke and criticism took its toll. You can encounter a major struggle with any subject on your own, but as to either mastering or understanding a solution, that is a totally different thing. It was only too easy just to side step and move on. Thus opportunities were often lost. With a teacher's identification of the problem, and the slightest level of personal encouragement, and support, the world of difference would have been made to me the struggling pupil. I can't recall any such encounter in my direction so I struggled on. I so desperately wanted to be awarded a prize. It just wasn't to be.

Rather than emphasize my weakness, I was desperate to establish a glimmer of positive reaction, often such acknowledgement invokes advancement. It used to be far too easy for pupils to be written off as hopeless cases. Teachers only wanted to concentrate on the top performers; or so it seemed. This action could blight a child's future and often determine the wrong direction taken in life. Some of us were slow learners, all we needed was a bit more encouragement. In fact, I'm not so sure that my analysis even now is correct-perhaps it was self confidence that was lacking. I had had the self confidence knocked out of me. We were still able to lead a productive and useful life, given a chance. Perhaps in my case it was necessary to create my own opportunities.

Hell! Am I introducing my excuses already for the manner in which this account is written? That's not the case as far as my interpretation goes. To be able to recall these early school encounters after fifty years is evidence enough of the impact it had on me. I have in recent years been able to communicate with four or five of my peers from that era; my recollections were confirmed: it wasn't just me. That was a very interesting exercise: comparing notes on how we had encountered fifty years of life from our start in post-war London.

What I'm trying to do is recall my thoughts and interpretations as best I can of events over fifty years ago. On reflection, I'm convinced that those formative years were of significant importance to me, but alas they were never developed in a constructive manner. This may well have been directly as the result of my own attitude. Selective learning was a key factor.

Nevertheless, I am convinced that in my case, it would not be difficult to sustain a convincing argument in support of the theory that ones formative years influence and indicate one's future pattern of development.

During our early years we were able to join the Boy Scouts which provided an excellent opportunity to develop our skills and enjoy our environment. Camping at Westerham and at Downe in Kent was full of great memories. The smell of the smoke from the camp fire, the watering eyes from standing to close to the fire and smoke. Crispy burnt offerings consumed with sheer enthusiasm. Trying to sleep on the hard or was it rain soaked ground. More often than not, soaking wet and covered in mud. I also feel that this period was instrumental in providing a sound basis for the establishment and understanding of the value of team work.

In 1955, I sat an entrance examination for the opportunity to attend a pre-sea training school. I attended an interview in Liverpool and was accepted. We were ushered onto a coach and driven to Wales the same day. I embarked on a three year training regime which set me up for a career in the Merchant Navy. Living away from home in the most fantastic environment was my idea of heaven. The college building overlooked the Snowdonia range. I had never imagined so many trees existed. My letters home often emphasized this point to the extreme.

Plenty of exercise and being well fed had a marked impact. I grew four inches in height and put on three stone. I was promoted and made Rodney division leader, and enjoyed every minute of the experience. During a three- year period I was awarded prizes for my academic effort and good conduct. What a turn around. I had found the key solution to an earlier problem. I found all of the subjects far more stimulating and they were now of great interest. It was apparent that I thrived on a challenge.

We learnt to sail in twenty-seven foot whalers in the Menai Straights, no mean achievement in itself, one of the most difficult locations in which to master the art of sailing, all aspects of seamanship, and navigation. We played competitive team sports, every day was a challenge. I was also the drum major and led the band. Swinging the mace with one hundred and ten percent effort. My determination to be the best never waned; sheer grit and the will to be the best prevailed. We often gave displays which always made a great day out. I recall that I was able to experience a distinct elevation in the standard of my performance displayed on these occasions. Such events attracted female attention. This was considered a huge bonus.

Every Saturday was liberty day which meant we were allowed out. Bangor was the nearest big City. We met the local girls and visited the cinema known as the flea pit. The police officer based at Menai, the village closest to the College, kept a very keen eye on us, reporting back the names of the lads fraternising with the local girls. He took his duty very seriously. My name was frequently on the hit list. It was all great fun and we developed fantastic team spirit. Outwitting the police officer became a weekly challenge and a great source of amusement.

The last prize giving was preceded by sports day. I was in a number of events including the long jump. Taking my run up, I took off and landed in untouched sand, it was the longest jump of the day. Only problem was I fell forward and dislocated my left ankle. I was conveyed by car to Bangor, ended up in Bangor Hospital emergency unit. The pain of the actual replacement of the dislocation was unequalled. I yelled and how. I had never experienced the like. My leg was then immobilised, plastered from just below the knee to my toes. I was unable to discharge my duties as drum major at the prize giving. This was without a doubt my greatest individual disappointment. After all this was to be my finale. I had been putting in a great deal of practice for the final show.

Nevertheless, I hobbled up to receive a prize. The lady dignitary presenting the prizes asked me what I had done to warrant the plaster cast. "I discolated (sic) me bleeding ankle, Ma'am" I said. Poor lady clamped her lips tight and went dark red, her shoulders were moving up and down, and she managed not to laugh at me. I was ushered off of the rostrum, leaving a number of people either struggling to conceal their amusement or seeking confirmation of what they had heard. (Oh that's not a spelling error by the way: that's the precise way I pronounced my injury).

We all made our way up and down Snowdon twice each year under the impression this was a character-forming exercise. Whatever the motive, it was always great fun. Not by way of the train I hasten to add, but on foot. Almost half way up Snowdon was a lake in which an RAF meteor jet had crashed some years earlier. The remains of the aircraft could be seen on the bottom of the lake. We were all instructed to strip off and take a swim. The water was ice cold every time, one hell of a shock to the system. After a quick swim, no one wanted to hang around too long. We then continued to the summit and back down again, all in our stride. We were all fighting fit. The whole environment was so much an adventure in my mind, which I thrived on every minute.

Every Sunday evening after tea would be a film show. The projector would be set up and the first reel would be loaded. Without fail, the film would break. I can't recall it being any different, and this ritual became a great laugh. The whole atmosphere was great; a lot of the lads were from children's homes. Having had a difficult start in life, they all seemed to thrive on the team spirit that developed. We were kids who were edging our way towards the door leading to the rest of our lives. Happy days we tend to remember the best whilst other periods fade.

MY DOORWAY TO THE WORLD

On the 10th October 1959 I joined my first ship as a navigating apprentice (Midshipman). The City of Leeds was located in Birkenhead docks where it was being loaded with its cargo. Having travelled to Liverpool Lime Street station by train from London, I made my way over to Birkenhead Docks through the Mersey Tunnel. I was so proud and full of anticipation, embarking on yet another step in a great adventure. I really had no idea what to expect; all I knew for sure was that I was going to enjoy every minute.

The ship was owned by Ellerman Bucknell Shipping Company and had been purchased from the Americans in 1947 for one hundred and thirty-five thousand pounds. The City of Leeds was earlier named Samcrest, a Liberty ship built by the Americans in 1941-1945 of welded steel construction as distinct from stronger riveted construction. Some 7176 tons displacement. These ships were designed for one trip across the Atlantic. During the war they became U-Boat fodder. 2710 Liberty ships were constructed during a four-year period.

The originally named Samarina became the City of Ely. All these ships were prefixed Sam in their original name; hence the generic term Sam boat. I would imagine Uncle Sam had some influence in the name.

Eleven knots on a good day, providing the wind was in the right direction. The captain's cabin and the saloon were air-conditioned but no other area had that advantage. In the tropics you melted. Whilst under way, the whole ship constantly vibrated and the stench of fuel wafted through every deck-level.

I was one of three apprentices and was soon part of the complement. We had a mixture of Indian and Pakistani crew, all totally foreign to me. Everyone I encountered on these ships was only too pleased to answer my constant questions. I seemed to generate a tremendous volume of questions on all sorts of subjects. This was a great opportunity to learn how people from the other side of the world lived and worked. I'm sure that my additional interest and questions enhanced the working relationship as I never, ever, experienced any difficulties with anyone. Sure: I learnt the hard way, and an endless list of pranks and jokes were played at my expense. The funny side was always easy to see and I enjoyed a good laugh. Being sent from the bridge down to the engine room to ask the chief engineer for a long weight was one of the first examples. After five minutes the penny dropped. As my confidence grew, I would get my own back, biding my time. We all got on very well, it was the only way, and a good sense of humour was essential. Contrary reports from my colleagues detailed the opposite attitude in the early conversations; winding up the youngest apprentice was a great sport. This was all part of my continuing education and experience which would prove to be of great value much later in life. The language and status had to be understood and adhered to; this was a totally new world where new rules applied.

My colleagues introduced me to Carlsberg and whisky chasers. After a couple of hours I made my excuses and went to my cabin. As I lay on my bunk the bulkhead started to spin around slowly at first. I spent my first night throwing up and we hadn't left the dockside.

We sailed for East Africa the next night. I was stationed on the bridge, recording by hand written notes in the log, the positioning of the ship as we passed buoys or navigation lights until we were in the North Western approaches.

I was then detailed to set up the log boom and set the log. The boom consisted of a solid wooden pole about four inches in diameter and some eighteen to twenty feet long which had to be lifted from its securing cradle and swung out to a 90 degree angle with the ship's side. The boom was secured and hinged at one end, with a further wire strop which provided additional topside support. Attached to the boom-pole was the log recording mechanism from which a wire to a brass-finned cylinder was trailed. As the cylinder trailed in the water and spun, the distance would be recorded on a dial which was fixed on the wing of the bridge. The back of the brass unit had a revolving clip to which all the trailing line was attached.

My effort to swing out the boom necessitated me positioning myself outboard of one of the life boats, one hand holding the grab-line whilst I leaned and lifted the boom out of its cradle with the other; in the one motion the boom then swung itself outboard, the sheer weight of the boom ensured this movement. As I hung over the side of the ship I looked down some thirty-five feet into cold black sea, as the ship pitched. I slipped and very nearly swung out with the boom. My seafaring career was almost over in a very short time. I never made the same mistake again; I enlisted the help of one of the crew on every future occasion whenever I had to perform that task.

I was tutored in all of my responsibilities from the start. My approach was one hundred percent: whatever the task, I was there raring to go. I was keen to learn, and learn I did, so that climbing the mast some ninety feet above sea level was not a problem. I thought I was fearless. Aren't we all to start with?

Here I was: heading for Africa, having previously never left the UK. North Wales had been the limit of my journey in life. I could not believe my luck; I was about to see the real thing. What an adventure and I was up for it. I didn't want to sleep in case I might miss something. I soon settled down and my expectation was fulfilled. I was taught to use a sextant and how to plot a course. No GPS in those days. If you had no sight of either the sun or stars, you guessed your position and just plodded on. Mid-day was positioning time when we would each make our own calculations as to the ship's position. Then the results were compared.

I did not have my own sextant at this time, but not to worry: someone would always help me by providing an instrument for me to use. In time, I became proficient by means of plenty of practice. The sextant was a vital instrument in producing a reading for the calculation required to establish a true position. I had a hell of a lot to learn, something new every day made life full of interest.

Our first port of call was to be Port Sudan; having experienced my first passage through the Suez Canal, the sight of ships moving through the desert sparked my imagination. The journey north to south through the Canal required an Egyptian pilot to be present on board to advise the Captain. I was instructed to go and prepare a ladder for the pilot to board. You need to be aware that the ship remains under way during this encounter. The ladder was constructed of rope about thirty feet in length with wooden slats forming the steps. If the ship was in ballast and unladen two ladders would be joined in order to make the required length. Having secured the ladder to a cleat I threw the ladder over the side. It clattered against the ship's side as it extended to its full length. Within minutes the pilot's cutter came alongside. Our pilot transferred to the ladder... (My immediate thought was 'oh shit, did I secure the ladder in the correct manner?' Not the time to be asking myself such questions).

I was relieved to see the pilot's head appear over the side and his legs swing inboard. My training had paid off at the nautical school. I had become proficient in the tying of knots and their uses. In fact I could tie all the knots behind my back at speed. Nevertheless, that first occasion when your proficiency is tested is significant. I greeted the pilot and led the way to the bridge, breathing a big sigh of relief.

The journey south through the Suez Canal required a twelve-hour delay at which time we anchored in the Bitter Lakes. This period allowed the northbound convoy of ships to pass and continue north, the Lakes being the only bypassing facility throughout the Canal complex.

Whilst at anchor, various 'bum boats', as they were called, would come alongside. These were full of all sorts of items: cameras, radios, watches, you name it; they would try and sell it at grossly inflated prices if they could get away with it. "Hey Johnnie you want to buy dirty postcard, dirty book?" would be a typical greeting. Whatever the purchase, you needed to haggle. It was expected by the vendor and the buyer and added to the colour of the scene.

I remember clearly my first introduction to the "Gilly Gilly men". These were entertaining; they had a repertoire of sleight-of-hand tricks. All were experts in deception and relieving you of cash. I was convinced that one guy was able to feel the surface of a coin with the palm of his hand. He then turned the coin over with the flesh of his palm without parting his hands. OK, he cheated but I learnt a lesson. It can be done and don't just believe what you're told and what you think you see. It cost me two shillings, as it was then, but that was worth the deal.

Having cleared Suez and our pilot having duly departed, we steamed on down the Red Sea towards our first port of call: Port Sudan.

My first ever footsteps on foreign soil produced an overwhelming sense of achievement. No longer exploring a printed picture in book or magazine this was the real thing. I'm here wow. Port Sudan, the home of the infamous warrior tribe of Fuzzie Wuzzies. The majority of the men are between six feet two inches and six feet eight inches tall, all with vast matted hair, teased with camel dung. All dressed in flowing, dirty, dark robes. I had never seen anything like this, not even in books. This was my first step into the big wide world. Wow! If this was the first step, what's to come?

The Fuzzies lived up to their fierce reputation and loud animated exchanges were the order of the day. It was extremely hot, much hotter than I had ever previously experienced. When the ship is under way, you have a constant breeze which is an advantage. Oh, so different in port. If I suggested that it was over a hundred and twenty-five degrees, I'm sure that I would not be exaggerating. Even the locals were keeling over. Our cargo hatches had steel girders with wooden section-boards which in turn were covered by tarpaulin. I remember having to jump onto a half-opened hatch. In doing so, I landed on the rolled tarp. Three Fuzzies were sleeping under the tarp. 'Bloody hell', it scared the shit out of me as I just struggled to stay upright and avoid falling into the hold. The noise that the three Fuzzies made was tremendous, arms and legs flying in all directions, they went ape. I started laughing and over-exaggerated the laugh; all three joined in. We all saw the funny side of the situation, I think. I just had them open another section of the hold and I got away fortunately with the interruption of their sleep. They thought I was fearless of them, having landed on the tarp and then got them working; mutual respect was thus established. Whilst we remained in Port Sudan, the three Fuzzies greeted me well. Although I had no idea what they said, they all smiled, so I guess that was a good sign.

From Port Sudan we then sailed for Mombassa, Tanga, Dar-es-Salaam and Zanzibar, then back to Mombassa.

Mombassa provided me with the opportunity to visit distant relatives. My grandfather's youngest sister on my father's side. My great aunt's husband, Arthur Beckley-Shinn, ran the East African Mercantile Company from his office in Mombassa. I was the first family member ever to visit. Arthur sent his boat to collect me as we were anchored in the channel off of Mombassa Port. His driver then took me to his house in Nyali. Greetings and introductions were exchanged, I met Zandra, the youngest daughter of the family, who was a year or so younger than me. She was beautiful, long blond hair, long golden legs; we struck up an immediate rapport. Suddenly we were told to hush, a familiar refrain crackled over the radio. It was the news on the BBC World Service, not a word was uttered until the news ended.

We moved into the dining room, which was set for dinner. Four servants waited on table, dressed in immaculate, long, white robes with the family's monogrammed initials on hats and left chest of the robe. My aunt announced that I should greet the servants in Swahili, the greeting being, "Jambo". I added "maszourie cabeesa" not knowing what the hell I had said, having just heard it said earlier in the day. My attempted pronunciation was the source of amusement. Zandra found it impressive that I already knew Swahili. I was then informed by my aunt that she had had a special meal prepared for me because- I was the first member of the family to visit East Africa.

She then clapped her hands and two of the white-gloved servants immediately lifted the silver domes from the serving dishes to reveal sausage, mash and baked beans. My uncle and aunt remained in Kenya throughout the Mau Mau unrest, in total some twenty-six years in East Africa. I really appreciated the kind hospitality extended to me, and our trips to the swimming club located on a beautiful white beach. The Indian Ocean provided an ideal location to swim. Zandra introduced me to her circle of friends and for two weeks I became the novelty and apparent interest of the moment. I lapped it up.

Having mentioned food, I should also highlight a major advantage in my view. Our crew comprised experienced seamen originating from India and Pakistan, in its self a volatile mix. Arguments were numerous, and heated on occasions. Our cooks were of Goan origin, Goa produces the finest curry cooks in the world in my humble opinion. Each day without fail, a curry of some description would be on the menu. This provided me with a virtual kaleidoscope of culinary treats. I interpreted this as an exceptional bonus, having never experienced the like in my life.

Some three months elapsed before we returned to the UK. Avonmouth and then Hull were our first two ports of call. When we arrived in Hull I was sent home on leave for two weeks. I would be notified of when and where I should join my next ship. As an apprentice navigating officer I was paid the princely sum of two pounds per week. All food and living expenses were covered. I started smoking and drinking just to demonstrate I was one of the lads and, I suppose, to experience what it was like. Before leaving the City of Leeds I had to pay my bar bill which came to a good deal more than I expected. Even to this day I suspect it was loaded by the purser. After three months I finished up with eight pounds in my pocket, and a wealth of memories. What a life it had been. Fantastic...

Having returned home, I probably bored my family rigid with my tales. My mum listened intensely about the feeding arrangements that had existed on the ship; clearly she needed to know that I had been fed well. My stories eliminated the drinking episodes; I saw no useful purpose in mentioning the numerous incidents. The discussions resulted in my mother promising to cook a curry for me before my leave was concluded. True to her word the meal arrived. Now remember, this was 1960, Indian take-a ways or restaurants, as we now know them, did not exist. Home cooking was meat and two veg if you were lucky, baked beans were regular staple diet, suet puddings padded out the quantity. We sat down to mum's special curry meal.

Could you ever imagine such an experience? The curry appeared presented on top of a rice pudding. Mum had cooked the rice with milk. What do you say under such circumstances? It was a disaster. With the effort that she had put into this treat, I could not let her down. She sat and watched me eat the meal in its entirety, whilst seeking assurance that her efforts were on a par with my experienced dishes.

To this day, my mother has never cooked another curry.

Sure enough, a telegram arrived for me instructing me to join another ship, the City of Ely which was loading cargo at King George V docks in East London. This was also a Liberty ship. On the City of Ely I was the only apprentice when I first arrived but I was soon joined by a young guy who arrived dressed in a brand new uniform. His name was Amir and he was the eldest son of a marriage between of Greek and Turkish parents. This was his first ship and I was to show him the ropes. Not a problem, we settled in and shared a cabin. We got on well together, a high priority under the circumstances. We set about familiarizing ourselves with the ship and getting used to the officers. The ship remained in London for a further ten days, during which time I returned home once or twice. Docks in London were going through bad times and strikes were frequently called. Ships were stranded, and the cost of the losses to the owners must have been phenomenal.

We were bound for the Persian Gulf as it was then named, via the Suez Canal. Our departure occurred during an interval between strikes and on a cold wet September night. I was eager to get back to the lower latitudes where the sun shone and shorts were the order of the day.

Amir adjusted well and dispensed with his initial superior attitude after a while and our relationship improved. We entered the straights between Gibraltar and North Africa and our radio operator received word of severe weather in the area. The chief officer instructed me and Amir to open the cargo hatches and to ensure all large items were secure and correctly lashed. This task took about sixteen hours all told and proved to be vital. As we headed East in the Med towards Port Said, a storm developed.

In my book, this was the mother of all storms with its forty to fifty foot waves. I was to learn that the Med was capable of delivering some almighty weather, the likes of which I have never since experienced. Amir was seasick immediately, he could not stand up, and he looked green, I mean green and the stench in our cabin made me retch.

Fortunately, I was not troubled with sea- sickness and I continued to eat every meal each day, the biggest problem being to remain seated in the saloon and holding the plate at the same time. With Amir unable to stand, he lay in his bunk moaning and looking terrible. I was instructed to be on a four hour on, four hour off, watch-pattern on the bridge.

The storm just went on and on for what seemed an eternity. It took nearly three weeks before we came out of the severe weather pattern; I thought it would never end. The ship was tossed about; it creaked and groaned; the noise was frightening. When I was able to sleep, I was just so tired I'd hit my bunk and I was out like a light. The motion of the ship just bounced you around in the bunk. It was never ending. The four on, four off took its toll; it was not conducive to rest. Ten days of constant battering wears you down. Add a further eleven days, and the fun is wearing thin.

One minute you were walking on the deck or in a companion way, the next you were tossed into a bulkhead unable to stand. You need to experience it to believe it.

The situation was so bad, that from the bridge whilst gripping hard any static item just to remain upright we had to call the engine room as the stern lifted out of the sea, so that they could reduce the engine revolutions; we were in danger of losing our only propeller.

Amir was struggling to keep water down; he did not eat any food for the duration of the storm; He lost weight and looked very ill. The stench was the pits. At last, after three weeks, the weather improved. I gave Amir a hand clearing our cabin and his bunk and we restored it to an acceptable aroma.

Gradually, Amir started to regain his appetite and colour. He wanted to go home; his career was over in his eyes. He confided in me that not only had he wanted to die, he was convinced we were all going to die. He had never felt so ill for such a prolonged period; he was clearly dehydrated and had gone through hell. I in turn told him that he was not alone, I too had been scarred, but we couldn't leave and had no alternative but to see it through, grin and bear it. I made no mention of the reputation of Liberty ships being renowned for breaking their backs; popping the welds; and splitting in adverse weather. The fact that they were built to do just one trip across the Atlantic in the 1940's backed up the reputation.

We passed through the Canal and then on through the Red Sea. Aden was our first port of call; we bunkered and took on additional fuel and provisions. The prolonged storm had taken its toll of both ship and crew.

Aden was not the safest of locations; we were not able to go ashore. Having taken on fuel, we left without further delay - after twenty-four hours. We headed for the Gulf. In all we visited thirty-two locations in the Gulf including Abadan, Khorramshah and Iran. It was still the era of the Shah. Basra, in Iraq, was the port at the end of the Shatt al Arab, the river which divides Iraq and Iran. The two countries were, in those days, in conflict with each other, Shots were fired across the river from time to time.

Whilst at Basra, we anchored in the middle of the river, the stern secured to a buoy and anchors used at the stem. Ahead of us was a Greek-registered ship which was in major difficulties. A spring tide, caused by the full moon, was powering the Greek ship uncontrollably towards us and a collision was imminent.

Our captain sent me over to sort out the Greek ship. I discovered that the ship was laden with jute which had been loaded wet. The jute had expanded, and there was also the added potential hazard of fire as a very real danger. Fire could ignite as the result of spontaneous combustion at any moment. The ship needed to be secured immediately. I explained the need to the captain who seemed to understand, even though he was under the influence of alcohol and was falling around his cabin. I'd caught him at a bad time. From what I could see, he was far from in command. I had to act fast; my instructions were to stop the ship drifting and bearing down on us.

I made my way up to the foredeck and took a chance. I released the anchor chain, which was made up of heavy metal links (I would have struggled to lift just one link of the anchor chain). The links ran through, and were controlled by, two adjacent capstans. I just released the brake and let the whole lot run out. I took the chance that the final end link was secured, there was no possible way to check. On reflection, this is why my skipper sent me: if I screwed up, my butt would be kicked. Luck was with me, there was no plop and splash sound as the final secured link fell into the Shatt al Arab. The additional weight of the links held and stopped the ship drifting. I called across to our chief officer who was standing at the bow of our ship waiting for my report. I'd let the full extent of chain run out. I couldn't see that any more could be done. The chief officer indicated I should return which I did.

The next day a visit from the Greek captain bearing gifts, cartons of cigarettes and two bottles of whisky. He wanted me to transfer to his ship and sort out the jute problem for him. A challenge I did not accept. That ship was in great danger of splitting apart at the seams.

I took the opportunity to visit Basra because my purpose in life was to see the world. In order to achieve my aim, I walked miles. The smells (or stench from open sewers) and the sights were so different, as were the people, the sounds. I took it all in. I didn't have a camera in those days. My memory was to be the only record. I knew that I needed to take a mental note because I was expected to report back to my brothers. They would be eager to know what I'd seen and where we had been.

We continued our journey around the Persian Gulf, visiting many States in the searing heat of the area. I lost two and half stone in ten months: the heat melted me. We all endured the conditions and made the best of it.

Daz Island was a memorable stop. Costains were constructing an oil terminal. Three hundred men worked at the location plus one woman, a doctor. They had an air conditioned club to which we were invited. The beer was cold and it was a welcome relief in the air-conditioned room. We drank our fill and more but when the time came to return to the ship the heat of the night hit us. As soon as we passed through the door of the club we were all hit by the heat of the night compared to the air-conditioned room. The combination of alcohol had a major impact; we were all pissed and staggered back to the ship which by this time was towering high above us, being in ballast with no cargo on board.

Planks of heavy timber had been lashed together and extended about forty-five feet to provide a gangway, no side protection existed. For some reason which does not come to mind, I was pushed to the front. I took a run at it, swaying from side to side but managing to maintain forward momentum, and made it by the skin of my teeth to the walkway.

Two of my colleagues fell between the ship and the dock and a sobering swim resulted. I'm convinced if they had been sober, serious injury would have resulted. I made it to my bunk and slept for twenty-four hours without waking. Several attempts were made to wake me, none of which worked. I was left to sleep it off. We sailed during the period of my extended slumber, my absence from the post I manned on the bridge when the ship sailed resulted in one hell of a bollocking and I was duly fined one week's pay, another two quid up my shirt. Sod it; it had been a great night out and one hell of a laugh so I'm told. I couldn't recall a thing other than running the plank.

I skipped the meals for the next two days or rather, to put it in context, food gave me a miss and I settled for a boiled egg which refused to stay down. Forty-eight hours elapsed before I could eat a meal or face a beer: sure sign of over-indulgence. With visits to Al Kuwait, Mino al Ahmadi, Bahrain, Bandar Abbas, in total thirty-two ports, we had spent a year in The Gulf. Bahrain was the one place I did not see. We were anchored off shore, and you couldn't even see land. The dhows came out to us and cargo was discharged into them. Our radio operator was sent home through illness caused by heat exhaustion, he had collapsed two or three times. He was replaced by a guy flown out from the UK.

Word came around that we were now bound for West Pakistan, India and Ceylon as it used to be named. My reaction was total enthusiasm. I couldn't wait to see what these places had in store for me. Another day, another continent or so it seemed. Progress across the Arabian Sea was slow but we enjoyed the weather; it was glorious. Day-to-day watch-keeping duties: four hours on, eight hours off, and little else. When on watch, and we passed other ships, out came the signal lamp (Aldis lamp) and we would exchange greetings and information in Morse code. I was also taught to communicate via low cloud at night using the signal lamp reflecting on the cloud, with ships that might well be fifty to sixty miles away, way out of direct sight.

I was awoken about 02:00hrs by one of the Lascars, his message, "Captain Want's you on the bridge now sarb." Captain Redhead instructed me to take a depth-sounding using the apparatus located on the stern quarter- deck. The contraption consisted of a drum containing an enormous amount of wire cable with a thin brass container in which a glass tapered tube, which discolours white, is placed. As the tube descends, and the pressure by depth increases, seawater is forced further into the tube. The tube is retrieved and placed in a box-scale which is then used to read off the indicated depth dependent on the colour change on the box scale. At the free end of the brass container, a lead weight is secured with a hollowed out bottom in which tallow is inserted.

Amir and I set the glass up and put the tallow in the base; this in turn enables a sample of the sea bed to attach itself. The wire screeched out to its full extent and we then had to rewind the wire to retrieve the glass tube by hand. The tallow indicated no trace of any particles; the tube was white in its full length. It had not reached the sea bed.

Reporting back to Capt Redhead, he laughed, "Of course it gave no reading, we are above the deepest known trench in the Indian Ocean. Good night."

Karachi, Pakistan, our first port of call and we commenced loading for home. More smells and sights: the poverty, these poor people, wearing what I would call rags, no shoes on their feet. These images were imprinted on my memory. There was also the manner in which they were treated by their bosses: beaten into submission.

The rickshaws were pulled at the trot by men eager to please; they needed the business. One operator would assign themselves to you from start to finish. He would wait for us if we stopped off somewhere. His face would appear from time to time, making sure we hadn't done a runner. Obviously just checking his fare was safe. Good communication was vital local knowledge and was so

important that the rickshaw operator was without doubt a
mine of information. Or maybe each of them had an answer
for every question, right or wrong. Besides, I didn't want to
miss a thing.

India was yet another world. I was issued, along with
the other officers, a drinking licence. Being a dry state, you
needed the paperwork. I still have the licence. Bombay was
a heaving metropolis; rickshaws were the mode of transport
here too. Tuc-tucs had not been invented at this time. Still
more smells, different yet again. The age of mass vehicle
transport was still to arrive. A marked difference these days
is the pollution that you can see which hangs over major
cities on the sub-Continent. One can almost cut the grey
cloud with a knife. It leaves grime on your clothes. Pollution
generated by failure to refine fuel to a clean condition;
total disregard for the health of the inhabitants and in the
interest of making profits.

Bombay, twenty-five years later, had greatly improved,
from what I had remembered. The huge volume of traffic,
tuc-tucs and certain areas which were established as well-
heeled neighbourhoods. It was great to see and witness
first hand progress through the passage of time. Such a
transformation; it was a treat to see the result of such
effort.

The sect distinction which was evident in India was an
entirely new concept to me. In my seventeen years, I had
never experienced any such thing. The class aspect became
prominent in cast issues; it was really the very first example
of racist dominance that I had encountered. It was black
on black and I did not understand, I was not impressed. I
drew comparisons with my own circumstances, which were
hard and poor, but what I saw in Pakistan and India was
unbelievable. Poverty to such a degree; I could never have

imagined the extent of such suffering. Deformed children were reared to beg; so many of them. At night, you stepped over bodies sleeping in the street; at least, I think they were sleeping. I doubt if I would have believed this situation existed if I had not witnessed it for myself.

Colombo and Trincomalee were the next stops.

Yet more intriguing sights in Colombo almost every corner you turned a new complex scene to absorb full of action and noise. My brain was almost like a digital camera storing these pictures. As we passed Mount Levinia, we had sight of a ship that had hit the coral reef. It just happened to be another Ellerman ship; the City of Ottawa had made an error in navigating the approach. Extensive damage had been sustained but fortunately they made it into port for repairs.

Sri Lanka {formerly named Ceylon} is a beautiful country with contrasting areas of fantastic levels of attractive scenery. The coast provides white sand beaches lined with palm trees, whilst in land, the vast hills contain the tea plantations. The air is cooler the higher you reach. The people are great: very friendly and colourful. I have always been keen to return.

Trincomalee, the stronghold of the Tamil Tigers these days, was a natural deep-water former Royal Navy base, with the jungle coming down to the water's edge. A stunningly beautiful location, one that left a marked impression on my memory and an urge to return some day. Some of the young women were stunning, natural beauty in its finest form as I recall, dressed in their silk saris, their dark eyes intrigued me.

Vishakhapatnam was the next port on the east coast of India, prior to the River Hugli and Calcutta. I thought my initial impressions were marked already. Calcutta took it to the next degree, bigger, more people, and the noise and, yes, the smells different yet again! I suspected the river Hugli had its influence on the smell. We used the British club in Calcutta, an institution from the days of Empire, with a swimming pool and snooker table. We had a great time when we visited and relaxed at this location. Four of us spent the day there and worked our way from left to right at the cocktail bar whilst interspersed with periods swimming to cool off. At the end of the day, we played snooker, a pound a corner was the pot. I potted the last four reds and all the colours in consecutive shots. Won three quid and I've never been able to repeat the performance since.

Whilst walking down Chowringhee Road in the middle of Calcutta, taking in the sights, I heard someone shout, "Hey Bazza", it was two lads with whom I'd been at school. That finished up yet another lost day, one of hilarious laughter and exchange of tales over a few beers or five... It was also at this time that I met Mother Teresa at her mission. This was long before she became so widely and well acknowledged for her work.

Our last destination was to be Chittagong, East Pakistan, and now Bangladesh, located on a delta which encounters horrendous floods and tidal surges every year. (Often, cyclones add their power to tidal weight). Our arrival was just after such an event. Bloated bodies were seen at sea prior to making landfall. As we approached, we picked up the pilot. The buoys which marked the shipping channel were gone but some could be seen in the paddy fields or in the remaining trees. As we approached Chittagong, I could see a Clan Line funnel with smoke drifting from it above the trees about a mile inland. Sure enough, when a cyclone had struck on 31st October 1960, this ship had a boiler problem and could not put to sea in order to ride out the storm. It was carried a whole mile inland into the paddy fields at

Shonai Chori. There it remained until sold to the Bengal metal Company for scrap.

I long believed that the wrecked ship was the Clan McMalcolm but I'd be wrong. Some eighteen years later I was in the Dew Drop pub in Eastbourne with some mates; I was recalling this sight as I have described above, when a guy tapped me on the shoulder and said 'Excuse me. I have been ear-wigging your conversation'; he then told me the correct name of the ship was Clan Alpine and he had been the chief steward on that very ship. My story had been correct but for the ship's name. What a coincidence.

Enough of my salty tales. Suffice it to say that I enjoyed every moment of my three and a half years at sea. More trips to South Africa, India and Australia. By the early sixties, the Merchant fleet suffered great losses due to dock strikes and the changes in regime. Containers were emerging as the new system of shipping cargo. Officer positions were not that easy to secure and my attempts to join the New Zealand Shipping Company failed. I was turned down. A change in course was called for.

A NEW DIRECTION

I APPLIED to join the Metropolitan Police Force and attended the Borough recruiting office to sit the entrance examination during October 1962. This decision had been reached in the saloon bar of the Tyrwhitt Pub in Brockley, south east London, in company with two other friends from the Scouts, Bill Venning and Andy Day. We all decided to join the Police Force at the same time. Bill and I both joined the Metropolitan Police whilst Andy joined The City of London force.

Having checked into my antecedents and cleared me as acceptable, I joined on the 7th January 1963 and, as directed, reported to Peel House, a Victorian building located north of the Thames between Vauxhall and Victoria for a thirteen week training course. The individual accommodation was wooden portioned hutches. After two weeks we were transferred thankfully to Hendon Police College where we remained until the thirteen week induction training was completed. Four of the intake fell by the wayside during the training. The passing out parade was concluded by a dance in the evening. Several of the lads were from further a field and had no partners; I had close ties with a number of nurses from three hospitals so I recruited the girls and they ensured a successful evening.

Our class captain was destined to become Chief Constable of Nottinghamshire in the fullness of time.

Details of our postings were announced and I, with Ian Loudon from Renfrew in Scotland, was posted to (MK) Kennington Road Police station. I became PC 450 M and the next two months were spent learning patrol-beats under the supervision of an experienced PC. More often than not, the tutor PCs did not want us trailing along with them, asking stupid questions. We soon picked up the operational standard required. I introduced Ian to the places worth visiting in South London as he was new to London and he appreciated the friendship. The majority of the guys on our relief were good fun to work with and we fitted in well. I must admit I always enjoyed working the beats around the embankment between Lambeth Bridge in the west and Waterloo Bridge to the east; all along the South Bank in fact. Tourists flocked to the area. I spent hours chatting to females from all over the world. Plenty of photo calls. I always enjoyed the evening with the lights reflecting off the Thames; a great atmosphere prevailed. I was proud to be from London.

We resided in Gilmore House, a section house, which provided accommodation for single coppers. Being close to Westminster Bridge it was handy for the West End. One other advantage with working from Kennington was that we were always in the front row for state occasions.

Another good friend who was destined to become one of Prince Charles's and Princess Diana's body guards was in our group of close friends. Princess Diana tried to match-make one of her friends with Jim. I visited Jim's parents at his invitation for a long weekend in Scotland. His father was an estate-keeper at a great location. We walked part of the estate with his father's twelve bore. I was carrying the gun when I spotted a movement; I lifted the gun and fired. At that point I mentioned to Jim that it was black but I had no idea what it was. Jim was most concerned that I may well have shot the estate owner's cat.

We soon found my target; it had been a black rabbit. Now destined to be a fresh meal for the dogs.

We had only been on division about four months when an annual event occurred. A list appeared on the notice board for names to be submitted for competitors for the Barking to Southend walk. This was an organised twenty-seven mile road race. My name appeared on the list along with Ian's. Someone thought it was a great wheeze to put us both up for the event. The only training we had was pounding the beat around Kennington and the South Bank. Not being one to turn down a challenge I left my name on the list.

On the day of the event, we set off from Barking in the mass start, my recollection still after all these years is the pain in both calves which seemed to arrive at the start then lasted for the full five hours until I managed to finish at Southend pier. A bus then took us to Southend football ground which was the meeting point after a bath. I wasn't able to put my shoes back on; my feet were blistered and swollen. By the time I got to the Black Prince pub all the food had gone. Still, a few pints made up for that.

An event that proved to be unique and most memorable for me occurred one Thursday evening when we paraded for pre-operational briefing. I was detailed along with eight other PCs and one inspector to go straight to the station van. These vans used to be referred to as a Black Marias.

We made our way to the Old Vic Theatre which was located on our patch. The van was parked in the side road, out of sight of the front of the theatre.

I just happened to be sitting immediately adjacent to the back door. The door opened and the inspector told me to follow him. We walked just around the corner and just stood outside the front entrance to the Old Vic.

We were joined by a plain-clothed officer who ignored my inspector and introduced himself to me as Chief Superintendent; he was Queen Elizabeth the Queen Mother's body guard. I was informed that the performance was about to end and HRH would be leaving shortly. I was to remain on hand whilst Her Majesty transferred to her car.

Fine, I had my brief and just stood there awaiting developments. Suddenly the doors opened and the Queen's Mother floated through the doors to the pavement. I saluted her and said, "Good evening Ma'm." To my surprise the Queen Mother said, "Good evening, officer." We then proceeded to have an absolutely delightful conversation. Unfortunately HRH, car had not arrived; this was great from my point of view. Our entirely spontaneous conversation was somewhat amusing, I offered to escort the Queen Mother on a bus or if we hurried we could take the Tube as her car was nowhere to be seen. We were both chuckling and enjoying the brief exchange which I was told later, lasted eleven minutes.

I noticed the Chief Superintendent who was standing in the doorway smiling in my direction; I assumed in approval of HRH's animated conversation with me.

The car arrived and rear door was opened. The Queen Mother tapped my arm and said how much she had enjoyed our unscheduled meeting. I saluted and bade her good evening.

The Chief Superintendent turned to me and winked and said, "Well done" as he entered the front passenger seat.

So this event became a treasured memory from a chance encounter.

Pounding the beat was not my idea of a career so I applied for the CID. Whilst Ian became a noddy bike rider. All of our first two years was   known as the probationary period. During this time at Kennington I was attached to the CID for a month. One morning, I was detailed to go and accompany the Detective Sergeant to Lambeth Palace where a series of thefts had taken place. We were ushered into a reception room where we spoke with Archbishop Michael Ramsey's wife, Lady Ramsey, and the Archbishops secretary at length. Three sofas were arranged around a coffee table. Details were discussed of the events in question and I duly made notes of the facts and figures. During the exchange, I noticed that the DS had developed a twitch which became more frequent. When Lady Ramsey offered me a second cup of tea I looked towards my cup lowering my eyes. My fly zip had split and I was sitting there with my trousers gaping open. The DS never took me back to Lambeth Palace again.

I then spent another month attached to the CID at Thames division Wapping. Most of this time was spent fingerprinting and identifying bodies recovered from the Thames. All good stuff and important foundation experience. At least, that's what they told me.

I was transferred to Brixton Police Station fairly soon after these events and the CID was to be my new base. I hit the ground running; the work load was tremendous; a normal working day was never long enough it seemed to me. The office was a constant heaving mass of activity.

What a fantastic grounding for my future career. You name it, it occurred in Brixton. The experience would be extensive and varied. I was not to be disappointed. I never ever awoke in the morning without an overwhelming urge to get to work. I thrived on it.

Within a year, I had made one hundred and forty-four major crime arrests. My fifth arrest was for a murder. An Afro-Caribbean had chopped his wife up in the bath and done a runner. I tracked him down and felt his collar, not a bad start and it brought me to notice.

I spent most of my time in a Q car (Lima 11) which was a plain, nondescript vehicle. Frequent car chases never failed to get the adrenalin rushing. Armed robberies were commonplace. Stolen cars and break-ins of all types. Brixton was a hard area and produced a vast-cross section of work.

Somerleighton Road, Geneva Road, Electric Avenue all featured in regular action. In some locations the attics were inter-connecting which meant if we were searching number 24 we needed to visit the adjoining houses as far as 20, 22, 26 and 28. All the tricks in the book plus more, I can assure you, were used on both sides of the fence. This is the way it was; I never ceased in enhancing my education at the University of Life, which was Brixton in the 1960s.

One summer's day in 1965 I was involved in the investigation of another murder. A sixteen year old lad had been stabbed by an Asian of the same age in a park at Herne Hill. We arrested the perpetrator and I was tasked with taking the victim's father to the mortuary at Southwark to identify his son. By the time we arrived at the morgue it must have been after midnight. The mortuary keeper was in bed; his bedroom was located above the entrance. Being a hot summer's evening the windows were wide open. I rang the bell and from the bedroom widow boomed the mortuary keeper's voice, "I fucking knew it the fucking Old Bill want to see the fucking body. Just as I've gone to fucking bed." The bedroom light went on "I'll fucking sort this c..t out". It was about four minutes before the door opened. As the front door opened, I kicked the door as hard as I could; the mortuary attendant was still doing his trousers up. I grabbed the mortuary attendant, by the Adam's apple and squeezed. I said to him, "Shut the fuck up or I'll nick you, (what the hell for I had no idea, I was mad), we heard every word you uttered, this man has just lost his son, where's your respect?" The mortuary keeper choked out a half-hearted apology and said," Sorry guv I was out of order."

The formal identification completed, the father wanted to be alone with his son. He came out of the viewing room when he was ready. We walked back to the car. What does one say under these circumstances? We were never instructed how to deal with such circumstances on the courses I attended. I just left the father to make the conversation until for some reason I said, "I know how you feel". The victim's father turned on me and said, "You will never know how I feel". He was so right, that short sentence has haunted me ever since. I'd screwed up big time and I knew it. I could only apologize, a valuable lesson learnt on the front line.

I was sent to the Detective Training College located in Chelsea for a six week course which was hard going but well worth the effort.

Brixton was an education second to none. I spent two years of the best time of my Police service at that station. Several commendations and one Commander's bollocking were all testimony to my efforts.

My duties included night duty CID officer, which encompassed coverage of the entire division. No mean task and always a full night's work. Never a dull moment. In the mid 60s, computers did not exist. Reports had to be compiled by hand or using the bog standard Imperial typewriter. The extent of my expertise was two-fingered pounding; smoke could often be seen wafting (or was it dust) from the machine at which I was hammering away.

Whatever the activities on the division at night, a full report needed to be left for the respective Detective Inspector whose sub-division was involved. The night duty shift started at 22:00hrs and finished at 06:00hrs. We always needed more time to complete the tasks. I was pleased to see the end of each of the two week night duty tours. I preferred the Q car posting and the action which ensued. I was a regular visitor to the Magistrates Court, the Sessions Court at Southwark, and the Old Bailey; giving evidence at trials was common practice. It did not just happen either; in those days we wrote our own legal aid briefs for each job. No mean task in its own right. We were in fact doing the job of a briefing solicitor but without the pay.

We had to obtain statements and then submit the paperwork to the Solicitors Department at the Yard prior to committal proceedings and trial. Sixteen-hour days were commonplace and vital just to cope with the volume of cases. I was privileged to work with a superb team at Brixton. The majority of my former colleagues progressed to senior rank in the fullness of time.

Malcolm, my middle Brother, also followed me into the Met Police at this time. He completed thirty-two years service and became a legend in his own right on Thames Division. We were brothers and mates. I could fill another book on what we got up to. Suffice it to say that we had more use out of the Commissioner's launch than the Commissioner did, with permission.

I met my future wife Angela at this time, a painful period on reflection, as she was the receptionist at the dental surgery I used. My chat-up sessions were often uttered from a partially numbed mouth. It worked; I guess she felt sorry for me. We married in 1966. By far the best thing that ever happened to me. I won life's lottery that year.

Ian Loudon married his long-term girlfriend Margaret in 1967; their first baby was on the way when six months later on Christmas Eve. Ian was involved in an accident. He came off his motor bike and died from his injuries.

At Ian's funeral, which was held in Renfrew, twelve of us from Kennington attended. Margaret, along with Ian's parents, told me that Ian was always speaking of me; he valued our friendship and respected me. Those words meant a great deal to me and do to this day.

I had lost a mate who was on the threshold of his life, a sharp reminder of the realities of life. I never fail to raise a glass to Ian, each 24/12. His son is now forty...

I was transferred to P Division, working from St Mary Cray with the Regional Crime Squad. Then I was posted to Farnborough as acting Detective Sergeant for six months. Then yet another transfer to R Division at Greenwich, Woolwich and Eltham. Woolwich was a very depressed area at this time. Criminal activities produced ten murders in one twelve month period, generating a huge work load. Long hours and low pay were not a very good combination. I had encountered a certain senior officer whom I detested, a dour Scot. As far as I was concerned, he was in a permanent alcoholic stupor. I made my position clear that if ever the wrong person had been promoted this was the classic example.

I had more respect for the lady in the canteen than I did for this senior detective. When my annual qualification report was produced in 1972 I had to visit the acting Detective Superintendent: none other than the said senior detective.

He made it clear that as long as he was where he was, I would not be promoted any further. I had refused to take certain action that he required in order to help a friend of his, a scrap metal dealer. This was his way of dealing with me, he was on a mission and I would suffer.

These people in authority had their boot lickers, informants that just wanted to enhance their individual positions. He was bent but I couldn't prove it. I wasn't going to be at all subservient to this bastard, let alone call him sir. In the early 1970s there was a mass exodus of mid-service personnel from the Metropolitan Police. We had been ignored in the pay award. Taken for granted almost, it seemed that being mid-service, you couldn't afford to quit. The Home Office got that wrong. Over three thousand officers left during that period. A wealth of experience that could not be replaced. I called it a day and resigned in 1973.

Just three months later that same senior detective I have referred to was prosecuted for serious drink and driving offences plus other matters. He was sentenced to a term of imprisonment. In my book, well deserved. I make no apology for greeting the news with some satisfaction. What goes around comes around.

A FRUSTRATED ENTREPRENEUR.

WE MOVED from NW Kent to Sussex, taking advantage of the mid 1970's hike in property values. We embarked upon a self-employed business route which was to prove full of trials and tribulations, in an unknown and uncertain environment. Having our first daughter, Vanessa, a typical three-year old, I now had different priorities: I needed to ensure our economic survival. From now on I would need to generate every penny from my own efforts to provide our home, food on the table, pay the mortgage, and the means to survive. Now I needed to make some money. The days of the guaranteed paydays were over.

Believe me it's a very different scenario when you need to produce a service or a product that clients want to pay for, and it's really a whole different ball game moving from the safety of a protected environment into the unknown abyss of self-employed commerce.

During the first three years, I set up two small greengrocery shops and sold them on at a profit. This provided the capital for me to pursue grander ideas.

Sovereign Medical Services Ltd was a concept that I had in mind. Based at Gatwick Airport, I provide a private ambulance service for expatriates returning home sick or injured. In total, I acquired thirty Mercedes ambulances, five of which were based at Gatwick. The others I franchised out to operators in other locations throughout the UK and based close to airports and major cities. The concept was sound but maybe ten years before its time.

During this period I employed part-time staff from Surrey ambulance personnel; some twelve years later Surrey Ambulance service adopted my concept of operation. The fact that I had employed future senior officers may well have been an influence (at least I like to think so). They knew from first-hand personal experience that the concept worked.

October 1974 heralded the arrival of our second daughter Claire a significant date because she was born on my wife's birthday. The new addition to the family evoked greater effort on my part to succeed in business, despite the prevailing economic climate and down turn in business coupled with high inflation. A new phenomenon presented itself. Recession. Recession was rampant and the implications were not fully understood. It proved to be a massive struggle which was no different for thousands of others throughout the country who found themselves in the same sort of circumstances. Many struggling businesses were destined to go under, with disastrous effects for the staff and owners of the enterprises. Thousands lost their livelihood and their homes.

As Air Ambulance Service UK I obtained a CAA operators licence which would not have been possible without the effort of our initial operations manager, Martin Brooks. His wealth of knowledge was paramount in the early days.

On March 10th 1987 we played a significant role in transferring the injured passengers with captain Lewry and his crew of the Townsend Thoresen ferry Herald of Free Enterprise moving them from Belgium to the UK hospitals.

Within three years we were also operating three aircraft as air-ambulances, contracted to major travel insurance repatriation companies. We were well located at Gatwick Airport to provide short notice response with our aircraft which were combined with our road ambulances to provide the full package in repatriation. Together with executive charter, we struggled through the early days. Managing to pay the bills, wages and bank charges as the interest rates escalated to 23%: no mean achievement amidst hyper inflation and unprecedented level of recession.

This was more like the action on which I thrived. The business grew in reputation and volume, operating its British Aerospace 125 800, plus its two Lear 35 jets and two Cessna Conquest turbo props. We operated twenty-four hours a day, seven days a week.

The BAe 125 800 was owned by Anthony Jacobs, the founder of British School of Motoring, later to be Sir Anthony Jacobs, having placed his aircraft at the disposal of the Lib Dems for the election. Subsequently, he was made Lord Jacobs. Part of our deal was to fly his family free for ten hours per month.

Anthony Jacobs was also the treasurer of the Lib Dem party. A very astute business man with a well proven track record, he could also be an arrogant and bombastic man, in the extreme. Fine with me to a point. I entered the operations room on one occasion when Martin, the ops manager, was holding the phone at arms length. I could hear Anthony Jacobs sounding off. Martin mouthed to me he's been ranting for eleven minutes. I took the phone from Martin and shouted at the top of my voice into the phone," Bollocks." I can assure you this was not my usual greeting or conversation opener. My intention was just to stop the ranting.

Anthony stopped in full flow. I then said, "Anthony, don't you ever speak to my staff in that fucking manner again. If you have a problem come to me. Just understand I do not take this nonsense from you or anybody. Good day." I put the phone down. Anthony Jacobs, now, Lord Jacobs, never mentioned our brief conversation again. Thereafter we got on fine.

With one exception. From 1982 I had been involved with Papworth Hospital in Cambridge and its transplant team. I assisted extensively with setting up the protocol for the retrieval of human organs to be used in transplants. This, in the early days, required the donor to be transferred to the recipient whilst on a life support machine. The ischemic time had not been extended nor developed with the required supporting drugs for any remote harvesting and transfer at that time.

We were on 24/7 stand-by and we responded without delay. Terence English, later to be Sir Terence, and John Wallwork were the cardio thoracic surgeons. Timing was always the paramount factor in these activities. Surgery would commence on the recipient, based on my timings which, out of necessity, had to be spot on. The donor needed to be in place in the adjoining theatre at the right time for the operation to be successful: no leeway, failure was never an option. A responsibility that we did not undertake lightly.

Anthony Jacobs had a planned departure at 10:00hrs one morning from RAF Northolt with his wife and two friends; the destination Elba.

We needed to collect a young lady from Northern Ireland who desperately needed a heart/lung transplant. I telephoned Jacobs at home and I asked him if he would consider delaying his departure for one hour in order for us to complete the transfer and comply with our CAA rules on crew hours. Jacobs refused to move his departure time. He phoned me in the morning and asked after the young lady, "How did she get on?" I just answered, "She died, we couldn't get her transferred in time, have a nice holiday." I put the phone down.

Jacobs and his party arrived at RAF Northolt for their 10:00hrs departure. I spoke with the operations at RAF Northolt too. By 11:30hrs Jacobs was jumping up and down because they had not taken off. 12:00hrs came and they took off Jacobs wearing his panama and a face like thunder.

G-TSAM was held over Southend for a further two hours before being permitted to complete the flight plan to Elba. People who walk over others and treat all they encounter like shit deserve a taste of their own crap. Jacobs had his on that occasion.

The young lady was collected and transferred later than scheduled for successful surgery. I had no intention of letting Jacobs off of the hook with a true report explanation of the positive outcome.

I received a letter from surgeon John Wallwork of which I'm very proud. In the letter he states but for my extensive efforts in those early days the programme would not be where it is today. I had felt so proud to have been a small part of the team; an opportunity that I would never have wanted to miss.

We moved donors from many areas at short notice, at times contrary to the law. Moving from one coroner's area, to other areas without prior notice. Common sense prevailed. As far as I was concerned, it was my privilege to be part of the team. Many people benefited from improved lives as the result of the ultimate donation by so many traumatized families. I offer my enduring respect and admiration for everyone involved in such a decision. It will always warrant the highest level of personal respect in my book.

A new phenomenon to me were the pilots. Great guys and a lady, yes we had the first female Lear 35 pilot as a first officer. One or two of the guys were, in their own minds, prima donnas who knew all the tricks in the book.

Yet another sharp learning curve for me. When it came to air-ambulance or transplant, the task was completed with the utmost professionalism. A great team and a pleasure to be part of the whole operation. Job satisfaction was always at a very high level. That was one hell of a buzz. I managed to create a formidable team of doctors, nurses and paramedics all of whom would make themselves available at very short notice to respond to an operational duty call. I have no doubt whatsoever that many people were saved from suffering and benefited from their expertise. Everyone pulled out the stops, without exception.

On the executive side, Nigel Mansell was a regular client along with his pal, Greg Norman. Pop star Paul and his wife Linda McCartney. Liza Minelli on one flight which was positioning to Nice requested fish and chips for her meal and it had to be in paper. We duly obliged, our efforts were subjected to a complaint from Liza; we failed to provide any tomato ketchup. She had a paddy over that failure. You just can't win them all no matter how you try. Many other clients flew with us and enjoyed every minute. Business people and Government ministers positioning to meetings; all sorts of activities made up the working day.

Our chief pilot was one of the original Red Arrows team. He was a character in his own right. Gerry Ranscombe had his quirks and knew all the tricks and more. A significant problem manifested itself which Gerry refused to address. I had no alternative but to introduce him to his successor. I never saw nor heard from him again.

The substantial development of the business had been brought about by the sharing of the equity, in return for cash investment in the company, with a partner. My partner was Comte Philippe de Nicolay; son of one of the de Rothschilds who also had other business activities in which he was involved. I was in control of the day-to-day operation and I provided a large percentage of the everyday business through my well established contacts.

Most successful businesses are established by hard work, trust and client confidence, all of which takes time. Sovereign Medical Services and Air Ambulance Services UK were both based on these principles. Our reputation from day one was paramount: we were as good as the success of our last mission; screw up and the result would be widely known in no time at all throughout the business sphere. It's just how it is and thus the reason we were always on our toes. When dealing with human lives, often in a critical situation, all aspects must be covered and checked again and again.

A flight cruising at 35,000 feet with a patient on a stretcher in a pressurized environment needs the correctly qualified medical team and equipment. You can't pop up the road or next door for a forgotten item. All eventualities have to be covered. Expect the unexpected and, sure, one day it will happen.

One repatriation from Peshawar was of note. We refuelled in Tehran and took off in a storm. A lump of ice the size of a tennis ball hit the port engine; the impact distorted twenty-one turbine blades. From the point of impact each blade was bent back ninety degrees. We continued back on one engine. A tremendous effort by the captain Alain George and first officer Peter Durnford. The damaged turbine blades cost twenty-one thousand pounds to replace. Not any profit on that particular job.

On another flight in one of the turbo props, this time over France heading south, we suddenly dropped a couple of thousand feet. I mean dived, all your insides feel as though they are coming up, you know the feeling. The whole of the Conquest vibrated then settled. The captain turned to us and said 'sorry guys we had to avoid another aircraft which was on our course heading towards us'.

French ATC [air traffic control] got it wrong but spotted the error just in time. Just as well they were not doing a crossword. Such an experience instils a new interpretation of a "near miss"; it suddenly has a much more significant meaning: near hit...

Cash-flow had been a major hurdle as with all businesses. With the aircraft operation most expenses were paid in advance. We operated a system where no credit was extended unless an approved client. Payment normally needed to be made up front, before we took off. It was the only way.

Fuel prices had escalated, bank interest rates had increased to record levels. The special relationship between us and the contracted clients was vital; it needed to be maintained in a stable condition.

Interspersed with these activities we still provided security medical escorts. One morning in early October 1988 I was contacted by Cynthia Halls from Isis House - more later about Isis. A Ugandan national needed to be taken back to Entebbe at short notice; could I do it?

An hour later I was standing on the tarmac about to board the Ugandan Airways 707.

One of the Gatwick handling chaps I knew came up to me he said, "You're not flying on this thing are you?" I nodded yes. "You're mad, always thought you were a clever sod but that's stupid. This is an accident waiting to happen."

"Thanks' I said, 'I just needed to know that right now." The subject and I boarded and we were airborne an hour later.

The back of my seat would not stay upright and the armrest came away in my hand. It was raining hard. Looking to my left I could see water drops running down the inside of the windows, the seals were leaking. As we gained height they stopped leaking, the pressure had resealed the units. Arrival in Entebbe at 07:00hrs was a brief pleasure.

When I arrived at the immigration desk, I was viewed with suspicion and questioned at length. My subject had cleared arrivals and was long gone. I was escorted to the Lake Victoria Hotel and confined to a room. A guard was sitting outside the door. The Minister of the Interior wanted to interview me. He was coming from Kampala to see me.

The room had a bed in which I thought something was moving or was I just over tired? I looked in the bathroom. Tiles from the wall were laying heaped on the floor, it was a mess. I turned the taps on, one worked - it dispensed a rust coloured liquid.

Shit, I thought, this is different. I switched off the light and grabbed the corner of the top sheet of the bed then flicked the light switch on and pulled the sheet simultaneously; three of the largest cockroaches I'd ever seen scampered from the bed. Oh bollocks! Just what I needed.

About 10:30hrs and three people came into the room, two heavies and one little guy with a scar from his left ear running down his cheek and across to the lower part of right cheek. That wasn't done shaving. He was the interior Minister and we were going to talk. A very suspicious little bugger, "What was I doing here and how long did I want to stay?" were his opening questions. He asked and answered his own questions in rapid succession. It appeared to me that he was clearly trying to demonstrate his total authority. Whilst he had some kind of agenda, I was not to clear what it was.

On the final approach when landing I had seen the old runway where burnt out aircraft still remained in situ from the Israeli raid on Entebbe, when the hundred hostages were freed. They had just constructed another runway adjacent to the original. Amin's regime of terror had ended but they were very twitchy. The chat or rather lecture lasted thirty minutes or so, my passport was not returned to me and he asked for my return ticket which he took. "You will stay here until I give you permission to leave" were the little bugger's parting words.

I left the room an hour later through the window at the back in the bathroom. The guy posted to the door was sitting on a chair well asleep, his snoring vibrated the door. I just walked from the back of the building through a line of bushes and there was a road. I flagged down a small minibus type vehicle which already had several passengers on board. It was going to Kampala. So was I; that would do fine. I jumped in and off we went.

The road was a dirt road with ample pot holes which the driver swerved around, constantly avoiding oncoming traffic in the same moves. Having passed my shilling coin to the driver, probably six times the regular fare, we then bounced along to Kampala. Two of the other passengers chatted to me. One said he was a university professor. At the bus terminal I left and wandered around for a while. I spotted the Union flag fluttering from a building about two blocks away and headed towards it. The British High Commission. I popped in and met with the second secretary and briefed him on the events of the day. The conclusion not to rock the boat, go back to the Victoria Hotel and go along with the Minister's directions. He was well known for throwing wobblers.

The secretary would keep an eye on the situation. He would let London know.

I took the opportunity to see Kampala. Plenty of signs of the ravages of military action, with damage to buildings, a great deal of activity from the state of the buildings. I saw Cecil Rhode's statue in what was left of the gardens. Then I needed a beer, it was very hot and I was dry. I walked into the first bar I saw, through the bar was a garden area where I sat and supped. A group of people came into the area, one of whom was the guy from the bus, the university professor, he came over to me looking for a beer no doubt. We chatted for a while then he rejoined his group of young people.

Two beers later the Professor came over again, he said, "You can fuck one of my students if you want, she has already agreed. She's a good girl, no problem really, clever girl." Gee, thanks, I thought. I had bought the Pimp Professor a beer and now look what I've got. This has turned out to be some trip. I declined the kind invitation and walked back to the bus terminal, found a bus and returned to the hotel, climbed back into my room through the window. I couldn't hear the guard snoring, he must have wandered off.

I left the room through the door and walked around the hotel. It had a large swimming pool, which no doubt in its day would have been most inviting, but that was then, this was now. The water was black and rank stagnant. I made my way to the bar and ordered a beer. I sat and waited for the beer to arrive. A hand landed on my left shoulder, it was the guard. "Like a beer?" I asked, "Yes; give me a big one" he said. We sat chatting and supping for an hour or so. The more beer he consumed, the faster he spoke. He finally disappeared. I didn't see him again. I met another English guy staying at the hotel who was working on helicopters at the military base adjacent to the airport. He briefed me on the hotel and area after a fashion.

My stay lasted four days in which time I visited Lake Victoria, went swimming and visited the dining room for meals. The menu consisted of eggs, potatoes and cabbage and coffee for each and every meal. The only exception being breakfast, a slice of pineapple appeared on top of the potatoes. I was told that I was free to leave on the fourth day.

I left the aircraft at Gatwick with a suntan and nothing else other than my passport and a small camera, which I always carried, plus my overnight bag.

My wife had been worried about me, I hadn't popped in for a while, had Cynthia Halls. My wife had phoned a number of times to see if I'd been in contact at all. The second secretary at the Embassy in Kampala had not passed word on as he promised.

The following day, October 8th 1988, I learned that the Uganda Airways 707 had crashed in heavy fog on final approach at Leonardo da Vinci Airport in Rome. The plane had gone down in a cabbage field. Thirty-one of the fifty-two on board perished.

I can't for the life of me recall having run into the Gatwick handling guy since our tarmac encounter. His prophetic statement had tragically materialised.

Our largest clients in the repatriation market were assistance companies providing back up and support to expatriates either working, living or on holiday abroad. The holiday repatriation market was an ever increasing factor as travel further a field became more popular.

This market was a growth area of which my company needed to be a major part.

Competition was keen and pricing was cut-throat, margins were squeezed. My strategy had been to negotiate contract pricing on guaranteed hours. Rather than ad-hoc charter price bidding, which in my humble opinion was fraught with problems. I knew that the operations manager had differing views, which he frequently voiced to everyone, other than me.

As a family, we were in need of a well overdue break together so during August 1990 I took my wife and two daughters to Florida for a holiday. When we returned and I arrived at the office I found that Philippe de Nicolay had moved into my office and taken over. My furniture had been moved out and been left piled up in a store room.

I was not best pleased at what I found. De Nicolay wanted to take over and have complete control of the business. I learned that the other two businesses De Nicolay had both failed. He no longer had his plush office off of Park Lane. This now made sense of his desire to have control of the Company.

So, after protracted negotiations my wife and I sold our shares to Philippe. He wanted to pay in three tranches which was totally unacceptable as far as we were concerned. Either the deal was completed with one cash payment in full or no deal.

The cash was paid, I cleared my desk. Having spent ten years commuting between home in Eastbourne and Gatwick on a daily basis I had accumulated a mass of items. I boxed up my chattels, and then thanked all of the staff individually for their effort and support. I was aware that two specific members of staff had urged Philippe to move control from me. I did not intend making an issue of the situation, that time had long passed, and neither of the two could look me straight in the eyes, the body language was enough; they thought their future had been secured with Philippe at the helm. The coup had been achieved and completed in their minds. I wished them both well and left. Time would tell.

It was the end of yet another era.

WHAT DO WE DO NOW?

A QUESTION that had, in a way, been thrust upon us to a large degree. Our bank balance was healthy but we still needed to have a regular source of income. The mortgage needed to be paid and our two daughters had to complete their education.

Part of the sale deal which I had insisted upon had been the separation of activities that I should retain. These activities could best be described as the service that provided medical and security escorts to the airlines and the Home Office.

The service had been long established, dating back to 1982. At that time, British Caledonian was in full swing at Gatwick. B-Cal, as it was affectionately known, was by far the leading airline of its day. I knew the B-Cal medical staff well and we often provided special equipment or escorts on aircraft. Whatever was needed by B-Cal, once their request made, it could be considered done with immediate affect. That's how it was that a great working relationship existed.

On occasions, a passenger would not be granted entry for one reason or another. More often than not the scenario would be a passenger had no visible means of support having purchased a ticket, landed, and processed through immigration carrying a carrier bag of papers. When questioned by the immigration officer, the passenger then stated that the purpose of the visit was to meet the Queen or Princes Diana. This type of statement was often the first indication that all was not well.

Refused Entry procedure then followed and the in-bound carrier was required to remove the passenger back from whence they came as soon as possible to avoid further costs. On the occasions these incidents occurred I would receive a telephone request to deal with the passenger and escort on the return flight. Often such requests were at very short notice; maybe the passenger became agitated when boarding the aircraft. We often responded with as little as twenty minutes notice.

Grabbing my own passport, I'd make a quick phone call home. Then it was air-side to collect the subject and off to wherever. I always carried an overnight bag in the car just in case. It was often used.

High-profile incidents occurred with these cases from time to time. Some individuals were suffering from a mental disorder, they may have stopped taking their medication; often the desire to travel became a predominant fixation and off they went.

Arriving at Gatwick somewhat disoriented, refused entry, did not always mean quiet acceptance. Some people became violent, hence the need for an escort. I know that B-Cal always put the safety of their passengers as highest priority. No passenger refused entry would ever travel unescorted on any of their flights.

Another factor which added to the number of refused entry numbers was a brainwave by an American operator in Newark. It was People's Express, an emulation of Freddie Laker's Skytrain. Only with People's Express you paid for your ticket in mid-Atlantic. The numbers of refusals escalated, the format was crazy and attracted a liquorice allsorts of clients for us. People's Express did not last more than a year. Surprise! Surprise!

My support operation for B- Cal came to the notice of the senior immigration officer at Gatwick, by the name of Barry Lipscomb. He was a legend who had a forbidding reputation. I had never met anyone who had a good word for him. He was detested by his staff. I imagined him to have achieved his exalted rank by default, a factor which has been confirmed to me several times since. Promotion had been the only way to get rid of him and my assessment was spot on, as I learnt many years later. Lipscomb ruled by fear. His staff dreaded crossing him. If he walked into an office it would fall deathly hushed. He crept around looking for victims and pounced often.

I was summoned to his office one morning. Having introduced himself to me, he then lectured me on his observation of my operation, concluding that in his opinion we were extremely professional and a necessity within the prevailing and increasing airline activity. This was just what I wanted to hear. We were on the same page and I wasn't going to argue with his verdict.

My suspicion was soon confirmed. Currently, immigration was holding a family originating from Somalia who had arrived from Germany, having already been granted asylum in Germany. An interview room had been wrecked by the family, and he wanted them removed. How would I propose to carry out the removal? I had an immediate decision to make. Do I tell him how to do it or should I play my cards close to my chest? Not having met Lipscomb before, all I knew was his reputation.

I proceeded to explain how we could complete the removal. The flight was a scheduled flight to Germany. I suggested taking the husband first alone, as he had already demonstrated his willingness to resort to violence. The wife and two children we could remove on the afternoon flight, so permitting a full removal within the one day.

Arrangements were set in place and we moved quickly to achieve the first part of the removal. The whole family, as I mentioned, had already applied for and had been granted asylum in Germany. They even had an apartment for their use which had been provided by the German authorities.

The family had arrived at Gatwick under the impression they could get a better deal for themselves in the UK. When we returned to Gatwick to collect the wife and children, the immediate reaction of the wife was to feign a collapse. We wrapped her in a blanket and carried her on board the aircraft. Once seated and with seatbelt secured, the children followed like lambs, they were fine. Upon arrival in Hamburg, a doctor was called to examine the woman, she was still feigning collapse. When transferred to a wheelchair, she was taken off of the aircraft to rejoin her husband and return to the apartment the Germans had provided for them.

Two days later, Barry Lipscomb phoned me and congratulated me on the manner in which the removal had been executed. I have to say that I found Barry Lipscomb to be a straight shooter and I had no doubt where I stood. That said, I also felt that if I had a question it would be promptly addressed by him. He did not mince his words nor hide from reality.

At this time, the North Terminal had yet to be built at Gatwick Airport. All activities were concentrated through the South Terminal.

I was contacted by a clerk at the Immigration Office located at Isis House in Southwark. Word had filtered through about my set-up. An appointment was made to visit Isis House and I duly attended. At the meeting, I was introduced to three HM Inspectors who were at the senior operational management level at the enforcement unit located at Isis House. Dave Ellis, Tony Smith and Tony McCormack (in the fullness of time Tony was destined to become Deputy Director of immigration), Here were three very pleasant guys, easy to talk to, all with an underlying sense of humour which soon manifested itself. The meeting was a probing assessment of me and of our service. It was apparent that word had filtered back from Gatwick. I can only assume such word had come from Barry Lipscomb or one of his staff. I was never told who, and I didn't ask.

During the meeting, I explained my track record and experience. I don't deal in bullshit, I speak as I find, and if I'm wrong or at fault, I'll be the first to apologize. You can't expect to get it right every time. I'm not sure whether they believed the Lear Jets were a real fact or a figment of my imagination, at least that's how it seemed to me. As I said, I don't deal in bullshit so it was their problem not mine. We progressed to the nitty-gritty after an hour or so of interrogation. The HMIs had to be comfortable with me, which I appreciated. The interrogation was good. As you would expect, these guy's had a wealth of experience and used it to good effect. They had at least sixty to seventy years experience of monitoring immigration between them.

My answers created amusement to some degree I guess, I used my CID training to best advantage. It emerged that HMI Tony Smith had an ongoing problem to which he needed to find a solution. "Have you ever been to Zaire?" he asked "No, not so far why?" "We have a number of detainees who need removing to Kinshasa as soon as possible. Would you be able to look at the feasibility?" "I'll look at the possibility and let you know what can be done." I didn't want to appear too keen and I had a nagging gut-feeling that I didn't have the full story. Why weren't the Met Police taking care of these removals, they were the experts? The meeting lasted two and a half hours. We then adjourned to the Red Lion pub just around the corner.

A few pints later, I left and returned home. Throughout the journey a number of questions were buzzing around my head. I needed to get some answers and an informal brief on the situation. I telephoned one of the guys I knew on the Met Police deportation unit.

The unit was a closed shop and all of the guys protected their positions jealously. They had a gold mine within their empire and guarded it well.

Staff were selected and appointed by invitation only. You did not apply; any application would have been futile. After the initial greeting, I asked three open questions. The answers were lengthy but, I concluded, honest. The phone call had produced what I suspected. The Metropolitan Police Deportation Unit refused to travel to Kinshasa. Zaire was a 'no go' zone for them. It was not a negotiable factor either.

Just what I needed to know, obviously the information was not going to be forthcoming from Immigration because they had another objective to achieve. With my desire to concentrate on these activities I had what I thought was another opportunity at my fingertips. I looked very closely at the logistics of removals to Kinshasa and I understood the Met guy's refusal, it really was a nightmare. Absolutely nothing fitted in the timetable without encountering long delays whilst awaiting connections.

The scheduled flights to Kinshasa were twice a week from Brussels on a flight operated by Scabie Air. Can you believe the name? It could not have been more apt; Scabby described the aircraft to a T.

Operated by Sabena, the 747 departing (if the winds were in the right direction) at 23:30hrs ish. Two or three hour delays were common- place if the aircraft was playing up. It took time to fix the bits.

I contacted HMI Tony Smith in his office at Isis House four or five days later. I gave him a run- down on the logistics of effecting a removal to Kinshasa as I saw it, bearing in mind the fact that I had no local knowledge whatsoever.

No further information was forthcoming from Immigration either. This was a suck-it-and-see scenario littered with pitfalls from the start.

By chance, I found myself in Brussels the following week. With time to spare whilst awaiting my Gatwick flight, I took the opportunity to visit the Belgium police based at the airport; several of the officers I'd met previously. I was aware of the fact that the Belgium Police regularly carried out their own deportations to Brazzaville just the other side of the Congo River from Kinshasa. The region being a former Belgium Colony, these officers were the best guys to brief me on the area status.

To summarize, the advice was 'you've got to be mad to even contemplate going to Kinshasa, it's dangerous in the extreme, and we don't go there'. Brazzaville is close enough. We put the Zaioise on the ferry across the river. The other factor, and by no means insignificant, is Sabena fly to Brazzaville, we don't fly on Scabie. The passing last words after I thanked the officer were amusing, "Hey English good luck you crazy bastard, let's drink a beer." Several Pils lagers later I made it to the last flight to Gatwick. I knew bloody well I'd be taking a closer look at Kinshasa, sooner rather than later.

Deportation from the UK had been, in general, the remit of the Metropolitan Police through a unit based at Holborn Police Station in Central London. The unit was the deportation and extradition unit. I had encountered several of the unit staff. Barry Smith, the Inspector at this time, was on speaking terms (when it suited him). If they needed a medical escort he was smarmy to us and knew where to come. Several of the others deemed us way below them and would not even pass the time of day if we met as we did at the check-in desk from time to time. Regardless, I always made a point of passing the time of day. If I was ignored I'd make some fitting wisecrack in a loud voice. Prats, I thought, why do they worry about us? I soon found out what the problem was.

Money the prime revenue source. They wanted to protect their empire. The established empire was of no mean substance either.

They were cleaning up with expenses travelling business class as a norm, and first class in a great many cases. Every job entailed one or two night-stops in the best hotels, when they returned to the UK overtime was accrued in no time at all, plus additional allowances.

Just one or two trips a month worked out comfortably. Selecting where they wanted to go, and when. Full control and manipulation of events was going to remain with the unit. A dream job if ever there was one. I was viewed as a serious threat.

The alarm bells were going off like crazy; with us on the scene, our removals were costing a fraction of the Met's charges. Yes, that's right, the Met charged IND. We were a real threat and needed to be terminated.

Heathrow Terminal Two, and later Terminal Four, were the offices to which our invoices were sent by way of best practice no doubt. Payment would arrive within sixty days if we were lucky or at least twenty-five percent of invoice payments. One guy made the payments but if he was away, tough, they weren't made.

A HEO (Higher Executive Officer) Cynthia Halls from Isis House contacted me with the first job to Kinshasa. The first of twenty-two such removals that I carried out within a year. It was an education.

Corruption was rife in Africa. It manifested itself at every turn without exception. Every official we encountered wanted paying, they all demanded cash before processing your passport on arrival. Another official checking health certificates asks for ten dollars. If you paid one then you'll pay them all, the word would go around that you're a mug. If you told them to get stuffed they didn't like it and they would try and intimidate you, but each time I arrived I was acknowledged and never bothered by payment demands. They only spoke French and I struggled but nevertheless got by. The Belgium Police added to the general insanity. On each occasion, we were the butt of their jokes, not a problem for me. In a strange way, respect developed for us and we made some good friends.

The Zaioise were some of the hardest individuals that I ever encountered. The more I saw of Zaire, the more I understood the reason why people wanted to leave to make a better life.

The Congo history highlighted the extent of toughness that existed. It was an essential ingredient in an individual's makeup just to survive and we witnessed it first hand.

When conversing, for instance, without exception they are loud and very animated, which can be intimidating. Yes, this is just as I had witnessed back in Port Sudan in 1959. Trying to achieve domination of the conversation would be success to their way of thinking. Domination achieved by the loudest voice and the greatest threatening gestures. A distinct pattern developed. I employed tactics that I drew from memory, it helped but it wasn't a one hundred percent success.

A good friend of mine had just completed thirty years in the Met and wanted to join us at Airline Security Consultants. I took him on a run to Kinshasa. This time I had a couple of items to deliver to the British Embassy. The removal went fine and we cleared the arrivals at the airport. Kinshasa did not have any taxis as such; you have to find someone with a vehicle, and then do a deal. As I mentioned previously French is spoken as Zaire's first language, not English, which makes it fun. Anyway, I found a car and driver and I suggested John should negotiate in Welsh for a laugh. It was so funny and we agreed a deal to take us to the British Embassy. The journey took a good forty minutes along a long dirt road which is full of pot holes. Either side of the dirt road are huts used as shops or bars.

Suddenly the car we were in dipped at the front offside and grounded to a halt. The wheel had collapsed under the car. I said, "John take your watch off and any rings drop them in your pocket. Grab your bag, we may have a problem; if they want your bag, give it to them." We got out of the car: five or six people approached, within a few seconds, ten seconds and there were thirty to forty people surrounding us, shouting and grabbing at us. I grabbed John and said "There's another car coming in the opposite direction; we need to stop it." Luck was with us; it stopped; we just jumped in and the driver hit the gas. He took us to the Embassy.

We stayed at the hotel for twenty-four hours and the Embassy provided a lift for us back to the airport. They had a group of military guys based there. The flight was around midnight. We were dropped off, and the lads went straight back to the Embassy.

During our stay, John made up his mind about joining ASC. I wasn't surprised he didn't see his future with us. He didn't want all that crap; it was an easy life he wanted.

Another trip to Kinshasa I must tell you about. This was just before Christmas so I contacted the folks at the Embassy in case they wanted any items for Christmas. A list came back: a Christmas tree, a turkey, pork sausages and blue stilton cheese. I did a quick shop and we picked up all the items requested.

I went to Asda for the cheese and I had them cut a full slice off a complete round of cheese, it weighed about four pounds. Some slice of Blue Stilton cheese! We completed the flight and I was in big trouble. The cheese was a bit warm and the whole aircraft reeked of blue cheese. I was told in no uncertain way not to pull that stunt again by the cabin services director. All the items were delivered and enjoyed no doubt. .

Regular trips to Angola included delivering bacon, cheddar cheese and pork sausages to the Embassy each time.

Isn't it strange what little luxury items people choose when away from home for extended periods?

No doubt our efforts were appreciated and the items were consumed with relish.

We also had to cope with the dirty protesters. If you cover yourself in faeces you won't be removed. A fair assessment, I never found an airline who would carry such a passenger.

Having collected a subject from HM Rochester one Sunday we had to position to Stansted Airport for a flight to Brussels. Rochester insisted on collection prior to 12:00hrs but our flight was not until 19:30hrs. The subject was lodged in the cells at Stansted Police Station. At 18:00hrs we returned to collect him. The orderly on duty said, "There's an unpleasant smell coming from the cells, we've got a problem with the drains." Nothing wrong with his sense of smell; it was on target.

Not the drains though, so don't call the plumber or the drain surgeon. Our man has dyed his clothes with faeces, it's in his hair – correction, and it's all over him.

The point was made, we missed the flight. Two days later he travelled in a painter's suit and smelling a good deal better.

We expected difficulties and were not disappointed; every trick in the book was pulled in order to thwart removals. We only dealt with the defined, Exceptional Risk individuals, those who had committed crimes or who were violent, who had attempted to escape, qualified for the definition. Positioning to the aircraft was always entertaining. Once on board and taxiing the subject's demeanour changed, 'what will I say to the authorities on arrival' became their paramount question.

Kinshasa was not a safe location for us, we were not welcome and having delivered our client, the last thing we wanted to do was make things difficult for them with the authorities.

We would shake hands, wish the client luck and they would disappear into the crowd. We would position down to Johannesburg via Rwanda or Lubumbashi. Night stop and return to London on the next day's flight.

All the removals were completed as directed, incidents occurred, but it was all in a day's work. The learning curve was ever longer and steeper. The pinnacle was never reached as far as my own personal philosophy was concerned. If you think you know it all, you will be caught out, as sure as eggs are eggs. We kept meticulous records of every removal. Full detailed reports were retained of each subject whom we handled for our own protection as much as anything else. It was the professional way to do the job.

HM Prison Haslar was the absolute dross. No not the Prison or the subjects detained there, but the prison officers. Ugh.

The place was full of militant reprobates in my opinion. They did not like us, and demonstrated their resentment every time we were sent to collect a detainee from them. We were left standing in the rain when we arrived. Or the duty officer had just gone for a meal. Waiting time would be, without fail, at least an hour often two hours.

Property was never available; the key to the safe was always missing. These toss-pots caused sheer grief for the detainees by with- holding their cash or valuables. Can you imagine how a detainee felt when he was being collected for deportation and was told he couldn't have his property, including cash that had been taken from him? In most cases, this represented their worldly possessions for all we knew. The staff had adequate notice of removals but ignored the fact, whilst pursuing another agenda. Greed.

An immigration liaison officer from Portsmouth was posted to the Haslar prison but still the situation did not improve. I often visited a cash point and used my own money in order to give a subject some cash to ease their situation. I made several complaints but the Home Office simply refused to take any action. Who the hell ran the place? Obviously these militants who appeared to be a law unto themselves ran the establishment their way. They gave Group Four and Securicor grief. The problem being they resented the use of the private sector services and boy, were they going to show us?

Every detainee we collected from HMP Haslar was a major problem. It was just too much of a coincidence. They all brought apples out with them, a sure fire indication that a razor would be produced next. These were single sided blades removed from issued safety razors.

Razor blades would be concealed in the apples or within the belt loops of trousers. Out they came, often between two coins held firm with chewing gum. This would then be held between the fingers in a fist shape. Or flashed while on the tongue. These incidents were planned and well contrived. More razors left HMP Haslar than I was getting hot dinners. It was a problem and needed addressing. You might well feel that implementing a stricter control over the issue of razors to inmates would be a simple prevention step. Not on your life, that's not even a consideration.

I sought a directive from Headquarters, Shit, that set the cat amongst the pigeons but, for God's sake, a decision needed to be made. I visualized the corridors of power and the clouds of dust from the suits evacuating the place.

By sheer coincidence, the only person I could speak with on one occasion was Colin Manchip CBE, the Director of Enforcement. He, for some reason, answered the telephone. This was just fine by me; you have a problem go straight to the top. If anyone has the answer he should or at least you would think so. Wrong! I explained the scenario, one subject with two razor blades perched on his tongue. If he swallows them, we are in trouble, if we take them off him and he is injured we could be in trouble. We were en route to Heathrow Airport. Directions please? Not to Heathrow itself, we know where that is.

"The razors, what do you want us to do?" Manchip went silent on me, scratching his arse and no doubt looking for wisdom." For God's sake governor, we have an incident developing." "Barry, I'll call you back." The Top Man needed time to consider, concentrating his mind, I couldn't believe it. Did he have any idea what it was like on the front line, you don't have time for contemplation. He has not got a clue.

Forty minutes later he came back to me." Do nothing Barry." he said. I didn't bother to tell him we had already retrieved the razors, the problem had been dealt with.

This was the level of Directorial decision-making policy. My arse! They couldn't organize a piss up in a brewery. Without exception it seemed to me that the thinking was, if they made a decision it could be wrong, so therefore avoid the issue and it goes away. That's perfect, we can't be wrong.

The guys on the front line in Immigration are in general great, with one or two exceptions, as in all fields. Most are well read, highly educated individuals doing a thankless task. Priorities become the next day off and when is pay day, a sad indictment but nevertheless true.

Frustration abounded, the amount of effort put into the job was completely out of proportion to the results. Over the course of eighteen years I spoke to hundreds of Immigration Officers, AIOs, Chief Immigration Officers, and HMIs on the telephone and I met a vast number in the various offices. The further they advanced up the promotion ladder the more remote they became. They lost touch with the real world, and decision-making became a major problem. Policy became a quagmire, constantly changing, and never properly understood let alone implemented.

Deportation, was a necessary, politically influenced action, but half-heartedly approached. With no one person prepared to grasp the nettle and deal with the need to establish a permanent policy, the quagmire was set to deepen and spread out of control, with policy differing from one office to another, no visible co-ordination prevailed.

How could an unknown policy work? It always appeared to me each assistant director wanted autonomy and to impose their individual interpretation on policy: a recipe for disaster.

One department would not speak to another due to internal politics and professional jealousy, a childish fiasco which frequently culminated in unbelievable situations which needed to be seen to be believed. On a number of occasions I commented, when I witnessed such circumstances, that I was under a misapprehension and thought they were all part of the same Home Office Department, so why no co-operation? Don't ask, you don't need to get involved, was the gist of the reply.

As the volume of business steadily increased I opened a new office based at Gatwick where I located three new Toyota Land Cruisers. I recruited staff and trained them on the job, there was no other way. We were even joined by one former member of the Metropolitan Police deportation unit. He was part of the team for almost two years. Until one morning when he turned up for at 04:30hrs rendezvous pissed. He had not expected to see me at that hour. I physically pulled him out of the vehicle and we parted company.

I accompanied each of the staff until I was happy to give them control. Several potential security escorts did not make selection. Former Police colleagues were a problem, four failed to make selection. Great guys, many years of experience but they were unable to communicate with the clients which we were dealing with. Situations can be controlled without using an 'in your face' threatening manner. Our immediate task was always to assess the subject, a process that took five or ten minutes or a couple of hours. It could and often did vary. Nine times out of ten the assessment proved to be spot on.

With our tasks, if the wrong attitude prevailed, you could create a massive problem. With former Police Officers who, having controlled situations for thirty odd years, all is fine. When it came to one to one and talking a subject down, instilling confidence and trust, all too often, in the space of thirty to ninety minutes, they failed. This was a new scenario to them, and it demanded new skills which had to be found, developed and adapted.

I was seeking the right crew and standards were set and adhered to. I had no intention of compromising at any level. We would be assessed on the basis of being as good as our last job.

World travel was a big attraction but the task was the job not the fringe benefits. Selection had to be spot on.

Payment from Heathrow ceased and a newly promoted CIO [Chief Immigration Officer] was tasked with monitoring our activities and making payments. A Lloyds Bank account was opened and instructions were issued for me to send copy-invoices to the Harmondsworth office. Marked for the attention of CIO Alison Woods. Whilst also sending the original invoice to the instructing immigration office. Sounds simple, do we have a system at last? Understandably the invoice needed to be authorized, this was pretty basic. I had absolutely no argument with that, but what should have been a simple procedure was a nightmare. This really epitomized the ethos of HM Immigration, why do something simply when you can screw it up?

As I mentioned previously, we established a service in which we would respond to a request with the minimum amount of notice. The task would be completed by professionally qualified staff. I paid my staff without fail within 30 days, a priority I set and always achieved. We all need to earn a living; we all have bills to pay. My team would respond to a request without delay, I completed the deal in the same manner.

Cash flow was a critical factor; we needed to be paid for our work within a reasonable pre-arranged period, thirty days was a target but proved unrealistic. Sixty days from the date of the invoice was acceptable and should have been adhered to. In the wider commercial world this would have been the basis of a sound contract and fair to both parties. Every effort would be made to make the agreement work.

The Home Office proved to be the exception to these rules every payment proved to be a major task, it was like pulling hen's teeth. Certified invoices would be lost. Invoices would not be signed off because the officer involved had eloped with a midget from the circus. Or the fact there wasn't a K in the month; you name it, we heard it, a book could have been written filled with the excuses that were used.

I felt so sorry for Alison; she had her work cut out invoking reaction from the various offices. Staff would be on leave, days off or away on courses, paying our invoices was low priority or not even a priority. We spoke regularly and met, the same topic featured on our agenda. One topic highlighted our conversations.

Regardless of Alison's efforts, the payment level never achieved the acceptable ratio. We never ever covered the invoiced figure in any one month.

A deficit debtor situation developed and steadily increased month to month. Not an encouraging formula. It seemed obvious this matter was not even being addressed, it was not a priority. No serious consideration had been given to introducing a format that would work. No one wanted to pursue the subject, let alone find a solution.

Staff selection was crucial and we needed to adjust to a variation of duties. We were being multi-tasked from various sources on a daily basis. Harmondsworth dealt with detained subjects who were processed through the Immigration Courts or Tribunals located in a number of different cities not just in London.

Group 4 and Securicor were the contracted providers of this service but refused to deal with any Exceptional Risk detainees. Both contractors had appalling records for this task; they lost almost as many detainees as they delivered. A Group 4 crew I encountered, standing smoking outside the immigration court in the Strand, had just lost one of their clients. He had had it away on his dancers they proudly told me, and went on to say that if a Nigerian detainee absconded they never gave chase, it was a waste of time, and they would only get assaulted if they caught them.

They lived in a different world. No doubt they are good people, just doing a job and that's it, paid peanuts and expected to show up and there it ends. Three crew sitting in the front of a transit van with detainees in the caged area at the back. I lost count of the number of detainees that set fire to themselves; self- harmed, used a razor or just walked off and caught a bus whilst in their custody.

Security on the cheap, and a token gesture. By no means all of the staff had a laissez-faire attitude. Heathrow Queens building and Gatwick detention areas both had staff of a far higher calibre.

The level of expertise demonstrated by Group 4, Securicor, and Wackenhut made it easy for us to excel in the area we covered. None of these companies mentioned above would deal with exceptional risk detainees. Which was fair enough, they had had their share of serious injuries.

All three of our Land Cruisers clocked up over one hundred thousand miles within eighteen months, which was a fair workload.

I replaced them with new vehicles within two years. They were always serviced as soon as the mileage indicated. Expensive vehicles but they proved to be worth every penny, reliability was fantastic, and they were work-horses. Apart from fuel, servicing, one set of tyres and windscreen wipers, costs proved manageable.

The vehicles were all maroon and we were recognized at the major airports and all the prisons. Even the detainees commented on the vehicles. Word circulated amongst the detainees and filtered back to us. We were regularly told that exceptional risk detainees would say 'if the maroon Land Cruiser turns up for you, don't fuck with them'. If it's anyone else its fair game and a good chance you won't go.

Equipment was always subject to extremely close scrutiny and rightly so, all items used as restraints were required to meet Home Office specification. Unless the equipment was correctly approved it could not be used. All staff were then trained in the use of the approved items.

The equipment included quick-cuffs, Velcro leg restraints, and anti-bite gloves. We all wore leather jackets, which again provided additional anti-bite protection.

Most common injuries our crews encountered were bites, our leather protection kept these to a minimum but not entirely eliminated.

Our corporate name was Airline Security Consultants Ltd (ASC) my name was in the forefront and I dealt with all operational aspects on a personal basis. I refused to ask any staff member to perform a task that I had not experienced myself. In my mind it was imperative to be aware of all the pitfalls. Local knowledge of the destination procedures upon arrival was essential basic information. Knowledge of the subject's antecedents equally vital, so as to benefit the safety of the subjects and their escorts.

The Secretary of State instead of airline or ferry operator was responsible for the majority of the removals with which we were tasked.

The individuals were either failed asylum seekers or illegal detainees all of whom had been defined as Exceptional Risk, the risk element varied and consideration had to be given to this factor. We always endeavoured to provide at least one escort specializing in dealing with the particular kinds of identified problem.

We never lost sight of the fact that we were often dealing with individuals from totally different backgrounds from ours. We respected different needs and requirements that people had, whether an ethnic or religious need. A primary factor to which we adhered was avoiding discussion of individual cases; we were neither briefed nor qualified to discuss these matters.

If a subject wanted to phone their solicitor or a friend we would readily provide a mobile telephone for them to make a call. Our set procedure was always to introduce ourselves by name followed by a full description of our proposed mission. Invariably, the immediate reaction would indicate the manner in which we could anticipate the day to unfold.

Carrier's Liability for removal, I have already touched on, with my reference to B-Cal and Peoples Express. To expand further, you need to understand that carrier's liability also covers ferry operators and any airline arriving in the UK. In the event that a passenger arrives in the UK without an authorized visa when required, or a genuine passport, the inbound carrier is held responsible. Fines are imposed on carriers held to be in default through their checking procedures and a penalty of two thousand pounds per passenger can be invoked plus either the cost of detention and/or the cost of removal. These costs soon escalate and can be a major problem to airlines. Every airline, whether scheduled carrier or charter airline, must implement the required infrastructure within their check-in procedures so as to identify and exclude bogus passengers. Failure to address these problems could be the factor which determines the official approval or condemnation of the operator.

HM Immigration has extensive legal statutory powers which they can utilize if the circumstances demand. A captain could, in fact, find his aircraft had been impounded for failing to comply with legislation or failing to remove a passenger they had carried into the UK. Not once in eighteen years did I hear of such an incident of impounding an aircraft. On the other hand, I could devote a chapter to circumstances which required such action but the powers were never used. The resulting interpretation was one of weakness and utter indifference; carriers would effectually give the vee-sign to authority time and time again.

My personal interpretation impounding policy as witnessed by me was that this is a complete and utter farce. Either we have laws and they are adhered to, or we open the doors and dispense with Immigration. The pretence of non-enforced legislation is a pathetic excuse.

I'm always receptive of arguments to counter my thinking and I would willingly change my mind if the argument convinced me of my failure to grasp the interpretation. Or the letter of the law. Who has the authority or power to countermand the law of this land? Second rate civil servants do so daily. Is this proper? I think not.

I rely on common sense to a large extent in my thought processes. I can't claim to be well read or academically qualified but I can argue my corner with the best and often common sense prevails. Is it me? Or am I the only person who sees a distinct lack of common sense demonstrated in this country? Resources are wasted, just written off with a stroke of a pen or with delete-key on a computer.

Almost eighteen months after our departure from Gatwick whilst watching the BBC local news, Comte Philippe de Nicolay appeared on the screen. The reported item was dealing with the fact that the Company had ceased operation and was going into voluntary liquidation. The news gave me no pleasure whatsoever. No one contacted me other than a finance company that Philippe had failed to pay, I had been the guarantor, so collected the bill.

ASC's immediate responsiveness, case by case, paid dividends. We were acknowledged as the top line service. I was referred to as the expert to be consulted in these matters. This status had been earnt over the years and was fully justified in my opinion. We maintained a one hundred percent track record. Three attempted mass escapes thwarted and five attempted self-harm incidents identified and again prevented.

I was required to attend Apollo House Croydon once a month to meet with the Assistant Director Paul Quibell and HMI Bill Patterson to be de-briefed. This arrangement was bullshit from the start. What they wanted was for me to provide them with a protocol for removals. This was evident much later when I read reams of my own words which had been claimed and signed by Patterson and Quibell. Not once in eighteen years, other than Barry Lipscombe, did I ever see any of the Whitehall or Croydon suits on the front line during one of our difficult removals. Common sense indicated that witnessing such a removal on the front line would provide a vivid source of information from which a protocol could and should have been formulated and developed.

At one of the monthly meetings, Assistant Director Paul Quibell indicated that someone from a larger Company had requested a meeting with me. The company turned out to be Reliance Security; Quibell was trying to broker a take over. I was aware of Reliance. I had recalled them being raided by Immigration and thirty illegal subjects being found to be working for Reliance. Clearly Mr Qubell had an ulterior motive for his attempted brokerage.

I met with the Managing Director ; he suggested that joining forces could be an advantage to ASC. He wanted to take us over but that was it, he expected facts and figures to be provided, he wanted our success explained. This was a probing, fact-finding exercise; no information was forthcoming from his side of the table. I wasn't at all comfortable; there was much more to this than I was seeing or being told.

Prising the suits from the corridors of power, other than to play golf or to go on leave, was an impossible task. I even offered to collect them from Croydon en route from HMP Pentonville to Gatwick. Excuses and deferment; the exercise of witnessing any removals was never executed. My point being that you can write and read all the reports in the world, but no finer example can be obtained than that of witnessing a difficult removal first hand. Many factors are encountered and dealt with in order to complete the task. I failed to understand how these senior ranking policy makers could recommend and then set out guidelines from their offices in this way. Operational protocol was and still is paramount; all front line practices need to be clearly defined and, from time to time, adjusted. No two missions can be taken as being identical; if you do so, an incident will occur to prove you wrong. Each person is an individual, reactions will differ.

Various destinations required adjustment in approach. So many important factors need to be considered, rather than a blanket generalized 'that will do'. That approach is wrong and breeds contempt.

One Sunday morning at 02:00hrs I received a telephone call from Gatwick. It was the duty HMI, Mrs J Munro, a very pleasant lady whom I had met on several occasions. Could I assist by attending the Medway Hospital as soon as possible, a Pakistani prisoner from HMP Rochester had slashed himself with a razor in an attempt to prevent his removal to Pakistan. He was refusing medical aid and assaulting the medical staff.

An hour later I walked into the Casualty unit and introduced myself to the duty sister. I was taken to a curtained off section where my man was laying on blood soaked sheets, the floor was covered in blood. This chap had cuts all over his chest, arms, legs and torso. When I say cuts, they were not token slashes; I'm describing cuts where his flesh was hacked about, a terrible mess. I've seen some sights in my time and I have a strong stomach; I'm able to cope with the impact of such sights. One can best describe it as looking past the initial mess and assessing what needs to be done in a cool, calm manner.

The duty casualty officer was an Indian doctor. He was not a happy chap; our man had traded insults and refused to be treated by an Indian. I drew on my few words that I recalled from my days working with Pakistani crews and greeted the patient. He was seething. It took an hour to convince this guy that he needed to be stitched and have a tetanus injection without delay. It was pure coincidence but this man's elder brother had been a boson on Ellerman Bucknall ships. Out of the blue we had a rapport. It took two hours for the repairs to be completed. Four hundred and thirty two stitches later, all administered without any local anaesthetic. He was discharged. I took him back to HMP Rochester where he went to the hospital wing. I told him that I'd see him later.

When I spoke with Jill Munro on my way home I explained what had taken place. The following Sunday I accompanied our man back to Pakistan. He wanted me to visit his family and meet his brother, which I did. They were all at the airport to meet us. I was treated like a VIP. They had been told that I'd saved him from the brink of suicide. His version, not mine.

Whilst seated on a British Airways flight bound for Accra with a colleague and a failed asylum seeker seated between us, we were in the back row, our normal location. We pre-boarded a normal practice in order to avoid providing our man with an audience to impress. Thus by the time the other passengers boarded, we were already seated.

Other passengers took their seats and stowed their hand baggage. These flights often produced an alarming amount of hand luggage, passengers wishing to avoid paying excess on hold baggage would just overload hand baggage, all shapes and sizes would be crammed into the overhead lockers.

Most flights to African destinations carried entrepreneurs carrying their stock in their hand baggage. Our man asked to use the toilet, but having been aware that he used a restroom thirty minutes earlier, I refused to let him move, He had a stunt in mind and I didn't want to be wrong footed. Sure enough, at the top of his voice he shouted, "I'm dying from urination, help me" he just repeated the phrase for the

next twenty-five minutes. He was playing to the passengers, hoping to be refused travel. We were restricted as to what form of restraint we could use. Gagging was, for obvious reasons, not permitted. We could do little else but sit and listen. This guy was the star turn and was generating plenty of attention. The CSD (cabin services director) approached me and said a bishop who was on board had complained that we were torturing this man and we should be put off the aircraft. Could I eliminate the noise otherwise we would need to leave. I asked the CSD to convey my kind regards to the bishop, thank him for his concern, if she would please invite the bishop to join us, we have a spare seat alongside us, and he could then demonstrate just how we should deal with this lunatic.

The wink and smile was enough, the message was transmitted, no sign of the bishop throughout the flight. As soon as the doors closed, our man stopped shouting; he didn't pee at any time during the flight. I had been briefed earlier that this subject had pulled the same stunt twice previously.

Earlier, when another Company (our competitors) had tried to remove this subject, he had asked to go for a pee. He then stripped off and ran naked through the aircraft. This action had not endeared him to the crew and he had been off loaded. Our tasked removal was our first attempt with him and proved successful.

I entered into a two year contract with British Airways to provide our service for them, signed the contract and sure enough we were called frequently. It took nine months before we received the first invoice payment. They required a 'gestation period' nine months to produce a cheque.

Each subsequent invoice raised encountered the same payment delay. After the twenty-sixth consecutive delay I issued a 'notice of intention', to wind up British Airways, which I sent to them for failing to pay their bills. It attracted a response and payment along with another contract. I told them to stuff their contract in a place where the sun doesn't shine.

BA contracts department works on the principle that every company needs BA's business so they then lean on the suppliers using their resources to fund BA's needs. It's fair comment to suggest that they even believe their own marketing spiel, 'the World's favourite airline'.

BA ground staff dispatchers and flight crews were superb in the majority of instances. I always pre-briefed the crew prior to our boarding, as did all of our teams, giving a full report to the captain and the cabin services director of our mission. After all the captain has ultimate responsibility for the aircraft. It's only right and proper that matters are cleared by him. During that five minute brief, we needed to demonstrate that we had complete control of the situation. This practice was part of our normal procedure.

Having flown over one million miles, a great percentage with BA, and several incidents occurred on BA flights where we were able to assist crews. Any such intervention was only provided with prior authorization; it was always appreciated and noted. An example I can quote is an instance whilst en route to Kingston, Jamaica with a deportee, a Russian passenger married to a Jamaican lady, a very large man, who had consumed three quarters of a two litre bottle of vodka during the flight. He was due, along with two hundred other passengers, to disembark in Montego Bay. The passenger was completely legless. The cabin crew tried to move the passenger and it was clear it wasn't going to happen. The crew needed to leave, crews changed over in Montego Bay as restrictions apply on duty hours and time was passing. I made my way up to the CSD and offered to assist; the offer was grabbed with open arms. I suggested a high lift vehicle should be positioned to the rear starboard door. The vehicle arrived within a short time and the door was opened. Together with my colleague and our deportee plus, a Jamaican police officer, we lifted the Russian passenger onto the high-lift vehicle, job done. The aircraft started taxiing as soon as the door closed. The passengers in the after cabin immediately burst into a round of applause.

Yet another Jamaican, mid twenties, needed to be collected from HMP Pentonville. This guy thought he was Jack the Lad. Full of lip and he did not stop. All of his paperwork was in a false name; he had no idea that we knew precisely who he was. He was so convinced that he had fooled everyone. To cut a long story short, he was wanted in Jamaica for shooting a Jamaican traffic police officer and killing him.

On arrival in Montego Bay, passengers disembarked, Kingston passengers remained on board whilst the crew changed. Two Jamaican police officers boarded the aircraft at the rear door, they both approached row 53 from either side. One spoke to our man and addressed him by his correct name. His cover was blown. He left us in handcuffs.

I always enjoyed dealing with Jamaicans and there were plenty of them. All, without exception, were street wise; it came with the territory. In my experience, they had a sense of humour: trigger the spark and the job became easy in most cases. Almost all of our Jamaican clients were involved in drugs; their bling was a fair indication. Most clients were known to other passengers on flights and our presence was known and often resented. We were under no illusions about our relationship.

On another occasion, with a colleague I attended HMP Pentonville to collect a Jamaican who had been in custody for some time. Upon arrival we entered with our vehicle through the double gates, then made our way to the reception where all of our business was conducted. The duty officer greeted us with, "and how many of you are there?" "Just two" I replied. "You'll never do it" he bellowed along with the loudest belly laugh. This guy is a giant and really nasty with it. He's on his way down from the wing now with eight escorts".

It did not take more than a second to recognize the challenge. I was a good nine feet away and I was looking up his nostril. A big fellow with hands like a large bunch of bananas. I immediately thrust my right hand out to shake hands and introduce myself. He started laughing, looking down at me." I guess this is little and large in the extreme." He just kept laughing. I put the handcuffs on him and we left. I swear this guy was close to seven feet tall and broad with it, probably 24 stone of solid muscle. I sat in the back of the vehicle with him. Within fifteen minutes I removed the handcuffs. We had a rapport, this man just needed to communicate; he had so many questions to ask and that was not a problem for me.

My impression was that his sheer size clearly intimidated most people and thus he was always automatically labelled trouble. This normally resulted in a confrontational offensive encounter. What I'm suggesting is that this then created more problems. Sure, when vexed he would be one bloody handful. I wasn't going to piss him off that was certain. We made our way to Gatwick, checked in and boarded the flight. Our new friend wanted to know how an airplane could get off of the ground. I explained as best I could and he seemed to be totally absorbed, he had never been on an aircraft before. He then asked if we could move to a window seat, he wanted to watch the take off through the window. The flight was not over full. We re-positioned. As the aircraft taxied and turned to the runway our man was glued to the window, completely transfixed. Once airborne, he turned to me and said, this is a miracle, the best thing I have ever done in my life. We chatted non-stop throughout the nine-hour flight. When the meal came round he ate four meals and he was still hungry. Oliver Twist had nothing on this guy.

Upon arrival in Kingston we parted. I gave him forty five US dollars out of my pocket. In fact all I had, to help him on his way. He put his hand on my shoulder and he said, "You're the first white person I can remember that trusted me and wanted to help me. God bless you man hey respect" as his fist collided with mine "Thanks man" he said, he turned and away he went. I felt that he had meant what he said.

July 1993 highlighted the potential dangers involved in the removal of violent subjects in a dramatic manner. Mrs Joy Gardner, a Jamaican, was in the process of being detained at her home whilst being restrained by three officers of the Metropolitan Police Deportation squad. As the result of a violent struggle, Mrs Gardner collapsed and never regained consciousness.

Sir Paul Condon, the Metropolitan Police Commissioner, suspended all deportation activities by the deportation unit with immediate affect. Our work load increased but not by a significant volume. We were already dealing with the majority of the exceptional risk removals. I sensed a distinct unease when speaking with Cynthia Halls, an HEO at Isis House enforcement. Cynthia was an extremely quietly spoken woman, mid forties, a mop of afro style hair. Abysmal dress sense but the first impression camouflaged a sharp mind and meticulous eye for detail.

The staff at Isis House relocated to much larger offices at Becket House, adjacent to London Bridge. This period proved to be different in a number of ways.

I was regularly contacted by the media for comment about allegations which were made. Radio interviews were sought on different aspects of deportation.

Paul Quibell contacted me and asked me not to speak to the media following the grossly inept mishandling of post

Joy Gardner under any circumstances. He had had wind of something else, no doubt.

It arrived in the shape of Trevor Phillips, who, at the time, was fronting ITV's The London Programme. He arrived at our front door with a film crew demanding to see me. Conscious of my instructions I declined to take part. Trevor Phillips telephoned my home number about twenty times. Each time I answered the phone in a respectful manner but still declined to participate. I would say at the end of the conversation, "No thank you Mr Phillips good bye" having referred him to the Home Office press bureau for comment.

Phillips then started kicking seven bells out of our front door with such force that rendering around the door frame cracked, he thought that this would invoke a reaction. He clearly was on a mission and wanted me to provide him with film footage which he could use. After a while the local police turned up and a uniformed inspector came to the door. We assumed one of our neighbours had called the police. We had not called them, our phone lines had been monopolised by Mr Phillips. As it happened, we had an emergency call button in situ, this was in response to known petrol bombing threats that had been made against us. The panic button was there for my wife and two daughter's protection. The origination of the threats was known and had been taken very seriously.

The uniformed inspector asked to come in and I opened the door and let him in. I briefed him and gave him a police HQ reference which he called; the immediate result confirmed our status to him. He confirmed that neighbours had been concerned for our safety. "Do you want to speak to Mr Phillips?" he asked. "No I don't" I replied. "How many more times do I need to tell him?" I showed him the damage around the door and said if this continues and he breaks in, I'll nick him for you. I confirmed that the Home Office had told me not to speak to Phillips, so there we are: I'm not moving.

The police left and so did Phillips in a blue Volvo estate. Apparently, Trevor Phillips used my constant refusal to speak in his programme or reply to distorted questions that had been doctored for effect. My solicitor wrote to ITV and complained. There you go, it takes all sorts. The London Programme broadcast invoked a reaction; we were hit by a wave of hate mail threats and obscene phone calls.

Sir Trevor Phillips, as he now is, seems to have adopted a different approach these days. I can only assume the side of him by which we were confronted was part of Trevor Phillips 'go get a reaction' stance. He no doubt achieved his goal, achieved his targeted position.

All removals for the South East region passed over Cynthia's desk. Never once throughout my period of involvement could Cynthia's paperwork be faulted, it was spot on every time. Professional 'Immaculate' sums up her effort. She always struck me as being a very unhappy person. Colleagues gave her a hard time, I know. Her family were Cape-Coloured origin and they lived in South East London. Cynthia took care of her mum who suffered from dementia; life was not easy for her. Sadly, I learnt of Cynthia's death from breast cancer in 1999.

We made a point of attending her funeral and shifted a few pints afterwards, just as she would have wished. Peter Moss, Kate Moss's father, had been an acquaintance and I contacted Peter to inform him of Cynthia's death. Peter joined us at the funeral. I mention this in passing as I fear Cynthia never really appreciated how much she was respected. So sad on reflection.

A request would come through for our services, our operations staff would allocate escorts and Cynthia's team would prepare the paperwork, all of which would be placed in a brown envelope. We would then collect the envelope, more often than not from the saloon bar of the Red Lion, where the majority of the staff would

be taking their lunch break. The Red Lion never closed. Maybe it was indicative of the tremendous workload that lunch time regularly slipped to four-thirty in the afternoon. Late evening, the same faces would be there, Cynthia constantly smoking, sipping her Pils and ten or more other staff would be in deep conversation in the bar. The Red Lion survived on Isis staff patronage, tucked away in a narrow back street, close to the railway arches, a typical London local boozer. The immigration service had its share, or may be above average share, of staff with alcohol related problems; no doubt the unsocial hours and immense work load were factors. Socializing was high on the agenda and rightly so. What better ingredient could you have in the make up of a great team.

Through the haze, the job was still done, and effectively so. Enormous frustrations prevailed, repeated unwarranted appeals and impossible lines of enquiry that cannot be checked." Why do we bother?" would be a phrase which was repeated time and time again.

Whenever I visited the Red Lion, I met different front line enforcement staff who knew of me but I was disadvantaged. I did not really know them other than the brief meeting. My personal reputation was built purely on achievement and my completed record of removals. From time to time, recommendations would be passed on which in turn resulted in a phone call to me.

I never lost sight of the fact that our operation was as good as the last job we completed. Screw up and we were finished and would just evaporate into a forgettable history.

Most visits to the Red Lion, and they were numerous I would regularly encounter a new Immigration Officer. Often they would want to discuss the feasibility of removals that were difficult for various reasons. The conversation would include in depth questions as to how we should approach the removal. I likewise would seek as much background information as possible. This was easier said than done. Cards were played very close to the chest; our briefing was not by any means always accurate. I would repeat my regular argument that at 35000 feet, in a confined environment we needed to know who and what we were handling. Screw the Data Protection Act, if an incident occurred we would be held responsible, and so we must be informed of any potential problems.

Colombia featured as a problem area. Bogotá was a different world. Danger lurked on every corner. I found Colombia very interesting and its history is intriguing. I spent hours in the Gold museum with its huge number of Aztec exhibits. Peru, was so different yet again. Lima provided yet more Aztec history. I was always in my element and would revisit the exhibits every time a chance presented itself. Nigeria was high on the agenda with five or six visits per week. Jamaicans were a constant problem, as were Indian and Bangladesh nationals. Probably topping the list was Algeria.

A large number of Algerian nationals were incarcerated in HMP Rochester. The flavour of the month was hunger strikers. No great surprise when an ethnic group instigate the same form of protest. Hence they became known as the hunger strikers of Rochester.

Forced feeding was not permitted. After a set period, the hunger striker would be moved to the hospital wing. It became apparent that the hunger strike was, in some instances, in name only. Mars bar wrappers were discovered concealed in cells. Water was also taken. The protests nevertheless made the tabloids.

Algeria was a problem destination for us. It was extremely dangerous. Over four hundred Europeans had been victims of fundamentalist bombs or shootings in three years. Security was non-existent. An Air France airbus was hijacked and destroyed at the airport, resulting in the withdrawal of European airlines routes operating to Algiers. The only carrier we could use was Air Algerie. The timetable was such that we could depart from Heathrow, arrive in Algiers but we could not return or position elsewhere. Our only option was to nightstop in Algiers.

The hunger strikers were giving cause for concern, endurance time was dwindling, the health of the subjects was deteriorating, and clearly the last thing they wanted was a death in custody. The Home Secretary at the time made it clear no more deaths of detainees in custody.

At one of my monthly meetings I was asked to remove the hunger strikers immediately, I wanted to know the precise status of each subject to be removed, this was essential. All Paul Quibell would reveal was, as we already knew, they had taken part in the hunger strike protest.

When asked a direct question, PQ would never directly answer but he would put a form of words together that meant nothing. He avoided making a decision and was a past master at it. After all, make a decision and you could be wrong, could be held accountable by senior suits. This is the game the suits play. A ridiculous self-protection posture which undermines leadership and the implementation of policy. This factor alone produced a shambles of a department.

I asked, "In the event one of the hunger strikers should be taken ill or, worse still, even die en-route, what action should we take?" Quibell said, "You're on your own, that's what we pay you for." All I was looking for was some form of guidance as to how the situation should be handled. None was forthcoming, so I took the opportunity to remind him that he might like to reconsider his answer, because at that particular time we were owed two hundred thousand pounds in overdue payments by the Home Office. So, in truth, they were not paying us, they were just running up a major debt. Not to mention putting us, as a company, under tremendous financial pressure. We were being used and stuffed at the same time.

The Algerian destination was indeed very dangerous for us; we needed to use an armed escort in order to transit from the airport to the hotel. Once in the hotel, we stayed put until returning the next morning with our armed escorts to the airport for our return flight. The armed escorts cost six hundred pounds for the return journey. They were off-duty local police officers moonlighting. On one occasion, whilst at the hotel, a bomb blast rattled the building, shattered the windows. The car bomb was just outside.

We removed three Algerian nationals together from HMP Rochester. The conversation was very animated. We had no idea what was being said. The conversation stopped when ever an Air Algerie crew member passed within earshot. What we did observe, were articles being hidden on the aircraft including one of the subjects trying to hide a ring that he had been wearing. The ring bore some kind of insignia which clearly was significant. My police training kicked in; as we deplaned on arrival I retrieved the ring and paperwork that had been concealed. My gut feeling was that these items were of some significance but would have given a problem had the subject been found with them by the Algerian authorities.

This was prior to 9/11. We all knew of the fundamentalists and their activities from television news reports coupled with press coverage. When we returned to the UK I delivered the items to Gatwick. The duty CIO thought they may be of interest to another department. He then detailed his bad luck, having been arrested for being drunk in charge. I have no idea if the articles found there way to the intelligence department.

What was obvious to us, and I do not have one glimmer of doubt in my mind, was the fact that we had just processed three Muslim fundamentalists.

I knew that the Home Office were in an invidious situation. The immigration service was desperate following the death of Joy Gardner, hunger strikers, adverse publicity every day in the media. From my perspective I saw not one shred of evidence of a co-ordinated policy where all staff were singing from the same hymn-sheet. Rather it was ad hoc and 'oh give it a try'. We assumed that each immigration unit, and over thirty units existed throughout the UK, had autonomy. No two units adopted the same format; each unit manifested its preferred format. Confusion? I know, I'm repeating the status but it just continued in this way, it never improved. Lessons were not learnt from mistakes over time. Whatever incidents occurred, no changes resulted. No, let's call it chaos; confusion under states the policy.

Parliamentary questions were tabled almost daily. Often the questions related to the number of removals being effected. The use of restraints figured high on the list of questions.

I was absolutely astounded to be asked to provide removal figures for each of the previous five years. As I have suggested earlier I, by, habit, always tend to qualify questions and demands. I wanted to know why we needed to provide these figures, "Don't you collate this information within the immigration service?" I asked. My questions were met with raucous laughter. You've got to be joking, we haven't a clue. We need the information in order to placate some MP. This was the first of many such requests. It wasn't a problem for us we were computerized and within eight minutes I had the figures detailed Country by Country destination. The PMQs were often generated from Barbara Roch MP, Jeremy Corbin MP, Dianne Abbott MP or the late Bernie Grant MP on a regular basis; whilst in opposition they always did a great job on behalf of their constituents. Such questions always required reams of paperwork to be generated. Perhaps reams may be overstating it somewhat. From comments made every time without fail I always sensed the questions were viewed as nevertheless a constant irritation.

Irrespective of the government being either Tory or Labour, the whole sphere of immigration has always been a necessary evil; neither major party has really seen fit to address immigration as a total subject. I suspect the political gain/loss equation has been the unanswered question. What used to be ethnic minorities have been transformed into ethnic majorities over the years in a large number of conurbations and, as a direct consequence, have been deemed to have become at risk if the wrong policy is pursued. Even controlled immigration would at least be an advancement. Any suggestion that control has existed is an outright misrepresentation of the situation... from either of the main parties.

Logistical differences within the immigration service demonstrate that the policy variations are prime examples of failure. Without a uniformed and informed policy being adhered to throughout the service, I failed to see how a successful protocol could be implemented. I can only speak as I found, of the circumstances which directly affected enforcement and in particular the removal of exceptional risk subjects within whom we were called upon to deal. No better position than up front where the action is. The weaknesses and errors could be seen clearly.

Prime evidence existed of empire building within the service. This in itself was totally counter productive. It was also clear that a huge amount of financial resources were just wasted by the blatant failure to collate and then co-ordinate information. Protectionism then became a natural progression which in turn undermined efficiency. As promotion was attained, individuals would continue to back away from decision making. No one wanted to be seen to be wrong footed, as a decision could prove you wrong. Avoid making one at all costs on and on went the same routine.

Frequently, I would be summoned by an Assistant Director or senior HMI in order to attend a case conference at which time the major difficulties would be presented in the form of an 'in the event' scenario. How would you propose dealing with these detailed circumstances? An invitation for me to set out the logistics of how the removal could be effected.

I learnt very quickly to reply in simplified terms which were completely remote from any likelihood of the need of authorization being required, for any action which would revert to the Assistant Director or the Inspectors. These people, in most cases, were more concerned about their next promotion and protecting their index-linked pensions.

The merest whiff of problems and the senior officers would abandon ship. You couldn't see them for carpet dust.

The protocol we implemented demanded a pre-removal visit to the enforcement office of the terminal involved. Every Exceptional Risk removal needed to be observed by the duty HMI or CIO. If the senior officer deemed it required, the removal would be stopped under his directions. The majority of removals would be initiated by another immigration unit remote from the airport. The hostile reaction this invoked was staggering. Open resentment prevailed, I would enquire if they all worked for

The same employer, e.g. The Home Office. The question fell on deaf ears. Clearly jealousy existed between units which added to the problems of getting the job done.

We were left to get on with the task at hand, which we did, making sure that we did not become involved in local or Home Office politics.

One incident which highlighted these circumstances I can detail. A colleague and I had collected a Colombian national from a London prison; we were due to remove him to Bogotá via Terminal Three at Heathrow. The subject had demonstrated that he was not going to leave the UK eagerly, in fact just the opposite. I made my way to the casework office at Terminal Three. The duty HMI was Bill Patterson, a Scot that I had encountered on a regular basis at Lunar House in Croydon. As I walked in the office, Bill exited in double quick time.

The withdrawal was so obvious and such an immediate reaction to my arrival. I was familiar with the reputation I had and that I should be avoided for fear that I might well ask a question

That demanded a decision. Two of the other CIO's were laughing at me and awaiting a wise-crack which I delivered.

I gave the HMI ten minutes then made my way to the gents toilet looked in and, sure enough, one stall was occupied. One pair of black shoes could be seen below the door but no loose trouser- legs. I said, "Bill, what's your answer to 19 down?" Back came the answer; he had taken to the crossword to avoid dealing with me. Enough to give me a complex of some kind if I'd allowed it to get to me.

Subjects due for removal but who were not considered to be high risk have, by way of normal practice, been sent letters from Immigration telling them to leave on a specific date and just collect a one-way ticket from the ticket desk at the Airport. I know what you're thinking; I did not believe it either, until I checked it out. Wagons Lits the company who had the contract for providing the tickets were in deep trouble over claimed and unused tickets, the numbers did not balance. Wagons Lits had a restricted period of credit, having issued the tickets, and then they had to be paid for. Slow payment by the Home Office created a serious cash-flow problem for them too. A very good friend of mine at Wagons Lits confided in me about this significant problem. The level of debt being forced on them was three hundred percent more than our figure. This information enabled me to run regular comparisons with our position. This was a clear indication how the Home Office worked.

No one in the Immigration service, to my knowledge, collated these voluntary activities. They did not have a clue who had gone or who had failed to turn up. I know for a fact that relatives frequently used the one-way tickets. It was generally known in immigration offices at the terminals but no one bothered. The old Brian Rix Whitehall farces didn't hold a candle to this farce to beat all farces. A constant haemorrhage of public money not small amounts either, none of which warranted any attention by the department. How can that be justified?

Woops! there I go again "Not fit for purpose" comes to mind, a phrase often heard bandied about along with many others which I classified as, "Speak of the day". "Best Practice", no doubt located somewhere is an office where "Speak of the Day" is generated; these phrases, often used with multi-variant interpretations. Always with an establishment get-out, being the final meaning if needed. I'm sure a descriptive word exists for such a phrase but alas I don't know it. If such a descriptive word does not exist, it should. How about suggestio falsi or suppressio veri {genures of verbal deceitfulness} ?

Exemplary paperwork, always 100% correct, generated by the enforcement unit at Isis House where John Eaton was the clerk working for Cynthia Halls. I know I mentioned this previously but it warrants the repetition. I would suggest that this was the only unit that knew and adhered to the format. Frequently units would screw up, and how. Subjects being sent back to the wrong destination. Dakar and Dhaka was a frequent error. How can you mistake the subjects from Senegal and Bangladesh? Nevertheless, Immigration could and did do it, not just once either.

Often passports were sent to Croydon, both Apollo and Lunar House, but nine out of ten would vanish without trace. A sheer stroke of bad luck? Of course it was. It couldn't be anything else. How many passports disappeared in ten years? Just a rough estimate: seventeen hundred and fifty. Do you think they had a problem in the building? Yes they did and it was dealt with after a long investigation.

Ignore it, it will go away. Issue a travel document. Paul Quibell's words are ringing in my ears, "If it ain't broke, don't fix it." My question, "Just how broke does a system need to be before you do fix it?"

Both Lunar and Apollo House in Croydon were due to be refurbished and updated in the process. All documentation files were to be stored below ground during the refurbishment. A workable idea, no doubt, until the air was found to be contaminated and files could not be retrieved. The underground storage became flooded. Woops!

Unsigned travel documents, travel documents with no photograph, no dates, incomplete information. Whilst I accept to some extent the scenario, our work load was heavy; no excuse warrants such flagrant lack of detail and failure to check. No wonder Nigeria and Ghana along with many other countries refused to accept them. They weren't worth the paper they were written on. All such travel documentation issued to us was double-checked as a priority.

Local Immigration officers based in receiving countries were not that enamoured with returned nationals or the security escorts accompanying them. Often the immigration officer would vent his spleen on the escorts. Nigeria was so bad in a number of ways; I guess we transited Lagos five or six times a week. The Nigerian High Commission would not issue us with visas. So we always travelled without visas, which then necessitated a quick turn around, flying back on the returning inbound aircraft. This exercise made it a twenty-four hour day whichever way you looked at it. I insisted that under these circumstances the escorts should always return business class rather than cramped up in economy. My request was approved and rightly so. All of us could be prone to deep-vein thrombosis with the amount of flying we were doing.

Nigeria, in common with some other African countries, was probably among the most corrupt. Lagos airport corruption was endemic, you couldn't move without an official in uniform demanding money from you, even at gun point. If you paid, you were marked; they would all hit on you. This is where I would employ my Victor Meldrew impression at the top of my voice. "I don't believe it." It worked; they couldn't get rid of you quick enough. Once pulled, this tactic was remembered, no further problems. When you couple these travel-documented removals with the cost of an escorted removal, airline tickets and associated charges, the overall costs were astronomical. Escorted removals to an African country, for example, could cost six thousand pounds. Arriving with an incomplete travel document could invoke a refusal to accept the subject, you would all return from whence you came. A complete and utter waste of resources.

At one time this procedure was used by units to off-load problem subjects. Refusal to accept a subject, then sending them back to the UK was fine; they then became the problem of the unit based at the port of arrival. Gatwick was inundated with such cases. Effectively dumped on them by other units. No doubt this is where the bad feeling emanated towards other units.

Actually Africa is a good example because frequently the subjects from many African countries had no original travel documentation. A travel document issued for a one-way journey was the only alternative. Other regular destinations required all travel documentation to be issued by its London Embassy or High Commission. Likewise, for examples, Algeria, China, India, Pakistan, Ghana, Nigeria and several other countries insisted that all escorts needed to be issued with an entry visa. This may well have been in order that the respective country could monitor who was being processed and returned from the UK.

Beijing became a regular destination; a group of Chinese had entered via Eire and made their way to Belfast where they were detained in a prison. None of the subjects could speak English and they all adopted an obstructive stance to removal. An interpreter called Mr Dong was provided for us just to assist with communication at the prison. It was apparent he wasn't generating the response we needed. It transpired he did not speak Mandarin.

What did happen, an event which made a vast difference, was the first subject that we removed wrote to his mates in prison and told them that we had treated him well and that if we came for them they would be looked after. His card was intercepted, noted and passed on to them.

We were tasked to remove a Nigerian national from HMP Highdown in Surrey to Lagos . An Exceptional Risk without a doubt from my brief. This guy was 6ft 8ins, a Nigerian basket ball player of some reputation. He had been pumping iron most of the time in prison. We made up a three-man team for this one as he had stipulated that he would kill one of the escorts if they tried to remove him. As far as he was concerned no one in the UK was capable of taking him. At least we didn't need to assess the situation: the status was clearly declared from the outset.

Upon arrival at HMP Highdown we were searched and progressed through to the reception unit.

The duty officer had already got a book running on the time of our failure to remove this guy. He said, "You blokes aren't going to take this one, we won't even mix it with him, he's dangerous." This was going to be a long day, no doubt. I was not disappointed. The subject arrived in reception with nine, yes, that's right, nine prison officers escorting him. The scene reminded me of the film The Italian Job. This Nigerian guy was the king pin and could no doubt handle himself.

He oozed trouble. In these situations, actions have to be co-ordinated, and spontaneous, telegraph an intention and you're stuffed.

I took the initiative and put out my right hand as if to shake hands and introduce myself. No, let's get this picture into perspective and accurate: I said," I'm...", our man bellowed a string of expletives, and his right fist and arm came towards me. I ducked and turned as my two colleagues put him on the floor. Handcuffs were applied in split seconds. He lashed out with his feet and legs. His legs were put into a figure four position and Velcro was then applied, thus negating any injury from that end to him or us.

We completed the paper work and transferred to our vehicle for the short journey to Gatwick Airport. The duty officer said, "Well that wasn't a text book departure but it worked. Have a good trip." We commenced our journey to Gatwick Airport. Apart from trying to sink his teeth into Paul's arm, we were under control. This guy hated the world and in particular he hated us. He cursed us at the top of his voice throughout the road journey.

Having cleared the security gate we made our way to the aircraft. I briefed the crew and we were ushered on board by the duty red cap (Dispatcher) the three of us plus our driver carried our man on board using the first class steps at the front of the aircraft. We walked through the aircraft heading for Row 53, seats CDEF; our usual location on these missions.

Once we took off, our man calmed down, he told us that his legal representative had told him to intimidate the escorts then they wouldn't remove him. So much for legal advice. Frank seemed to strike up a rapport with our friend so we left him to it. This can happen, so rather than interject, unless we were spoken to, Paul and I butted out.

Upon arrival in Lagos we waited for the other passengers to deplane. Then we walked our man through the aircraft. As we approached each steward or stewardess, our man cleared his nose and throat and spat at each crew member. We had our hands full and could do nothing. Someone was going to get hurt even yet. He wanted to leave his mark and no one would get in his way. This guy was evil and he was determined to show us. You could see it coming.

The Nigerian police officer at the door of the aircraft greeted our man and told him to follow him. Once off the aircraft we had no jurisdiction whatsoever. As he left, we thought it was all over. Wrong! Suddenly this din commenced, our man was running back to the aircraft, towards us. I was in the front once again; Paul was immediately behind me and Frank was behind him.

Crash, crash, crash the noise increased as he hurtled closer towards us along the air bridge. He was coming back for more. Yelling expletives at the top of his voice. The first punch came at me. I ducked yet again and he hit Paul in the forehead with an almighty crunch. I landed an uppercut amongst his meat and two veg from my very low position, which had the effect of removing the spring out of his step, but little else. I found myself half on the floor of the aircraft between this guy's legs, facing the wrong way. Somehow I managed to keep his legs still. Frank grabbed an arm and Paul, still reeling from the impact of the punch, managed to lock onto the other arm. I can't recall what I grabbed but our man left the aircraft finally to our relief and the relief of the crew. By this time the whole crew were gathered together watching the spectacle of these proceedings. The crew report would have made interesting reading no doubt. I know one or two of the young ladies had found the whole episode upsetting but the final departure and the spitting had emphasized to them that escorted procedure was in both their own and the passengers' interests. They told us precisely that.

Paul was in no doubt that two inches lower and his nose would have been broken and spread over his face, he had seen stars when the punch had landed. The noise on contact had been loud enough, I agreed, and had no argument with his assessment. We all slept throughout the return flight. That was one big bugger that we didn't want to meet again.

As to who won the bet at Highdown I never found out. When on subsequent occasions we visited the prison, a glimmer of respect prevailed. Our departure entered into the realms of chat over tea, no doubt thus we became known for our effective modus operandi.

By no means was every individual with whom we came into contact of, a violent disposition, although the majority were. Another Nigerian national that we were tasked to remove had been in London for some time as an over-stayer. He had been quite an entrepreneur during his stay, using a false identity. His efforts had achieved the exalted position of Director of Property in charge of Southwark's housing department. This event is easily recalled due to the fact that when we collected him from HM Prison Pentonville his baggage included a briefcase containing over two hundred and fifty thousand pounds in cash. No wonder he felt good about the generosity of the British system. When I questioned the fact that all this cash could be the proceeds of crime, the response was just let him have it, if that's what it takes to get rid of him. When you also take into consideration the fact that the Secretary of State was providing this individual with his free airline ticket home, the rationale was somewhat difficult to follow.

In fairness I must point out that recent legislation has now provided powers of seizure and confiscation of proceeds of crime. Such specific powers did not exist at the time of the events I have related above.

DSS fraud figured high on the popularity list of activities. A large proportion of the female deportees were convicted DSS multi-identity fraudsters. They were not meek and mild either; they could fight and bite: a face full of phlegm often accompanied a high octane tirade of abuse directed at the escorts. As security escorts we were tested daily in the most objectionable manner. A simple cure for the spitting or biting would have been the use of a face mask (such as paint-sprayer's use). Such requests were vetoed by HQ: yet another prime example of failure to comprehend front line difficulties. Front line observation would have been ideal evidence of the need for such preventative measures.

No one would make the effort to attend; such was the lack of enthusiasm for a constructive approach and the overall acceptance of responsibility to set guide lines. The outbursts I refer to always occurred in front of an audience for maximum impact. The ulterior motive being to try and invoke the airline's refusal to allow the subject to travel on the flight, and prevent subsequent removal. Likewise the drug smugglers (mules) the swallowers could be very difficult to handle. Often they had to be desperate people putting their lives at such risk. Hard as nails. Could they fight? Just don't get in the way of a fist was an early lesson we all experienced.

Deportation followed completion of their prison sentence. Collection from HMP Holloway was the precursor to an interesting day. We always had female escorts in attendance with a female subject, an essential requirement.

I recall one Jamaican young lady we collected from Holloway; she was a well known Yardie and had no intention of returning to Jamaica. She was located in the segregation unit due to her violent behaviour. The duty officer took us to her cell where, as soon as she saw us, she stripped. Three minutes later we were all in the vehicle heading out of the prison. Our new passenger was hand-cuffed for our protection as well as hers. Before we had left North London postal district this lady was out of the cuffs. She was double-jointed and could slip them with ease. This lady was built on a strong frame and was as hard as nails. Street-wise would be an understatement. She wrote the book. If ever the occasion demanded a sense of humour this was such a time. As it transpired, the format was right. We completed the flight without incident. Cleared arrivals and we made our way to the Morgan Harbour Hotel for the night. Little did we know that our lady had bribed an official and duly returned to the UK on the same aircraft. Three days later we returned with her yet again. She stayed in Jamaica for how long, I wonder?

The monthly debriefing meetings at Lunar House continued; average duration being an hour. Agendas were almost standard. Meetings consisted of an Assistant Director Paul Quibell, one HMI, Bill Patterson, one CIO taking notes (who ever were unlucky enough to be posted to the procurement unit at the time) and I. The CIO changed regularly.

Quibell had an ongoing problem, he couldn't sit down for long periods, and he was always in the middle of something else, excused himself and left the meeting to Bill Patterson. I'm convinced in retrospect that this was avoidance of policy-making decisions and awkward questions.

During 1996 I was requested to provide additional information over and above the usual annual staff qualification certificates. All of our staff were professionally qualified; they held first aid certificates which had to be current in addition to their state RGN or RMN qualifications. Also certification in control and restraint training. Questions were asked about how we obtained air-side insurance. Which department issued our vehicle air-side passes?

I wasn't comfortable with the manner they were trying to extract this information. In fact all the information could be obtained relatively quickly with a number of phone calls. They wanted the names of my BAA contacts in the security departments.

I declined to reveal all the information until they told me what was going on.

Quibell told me that he wanted to bring another company on line, the company being Loss Prevention International Ltd based in Aldershot Hampshire.

My reaction fine, not a problem, at least we now know what's happening; it will keep us on our toes. I then raised the old chestnut of late payment yet again. At this stage the indebtedness had escalated to over four-hundred thousand pounds, serious money. My patience was rapidly evaporating. No company could be expected to carry this level of late payments. It was a recipe for commercial disaster. I once again produced documentation as support evidence. It was clear that not one month had passed when the Home Office had paid bills, which amounted to a figure that exceeded the invoiced amount for the same month. It's not rocket science to work out what was happening.

Now they wanted another sucker onto whom to spread the debt.

Our operational protocol stipulated pre-boarding of subjects in order to minimize inconvenience to other passengers. This also served to provide reassurance to the captain and crew that we had the situation under control. In their position, I too would have wanted such confirmation.

Flying in a pressurized aircraft at 39000 feet for five to ten hours duration, with over 300 passengers plus crew and one individual with known questionable behaviour problems is not to be recommended. Things do go wrong and the consequences can be fatal.

The Belgium police were deporting a violent female on a Sabena flight to Brazzaville. During the flight a violent episode occurred during which time the woman had to be restrained. It transpired that the woman sustained a heart attack and died. Tragic in the extreme and stark warning. A startling reminder of the fine line which could change circumstances in an instant.

Whenever our services were requested the request was fully justified and authorized by a senior immigration officer. Not every mission resulted in an incident thankfully. I would like to think that such incidents were limited as the result of the teamwork combined with individual expertise, demonstrated by each and every team member.

Respect for each and every person we encountered was an essential ingredient which would be sorely tested to the extreme with regular monotony. Each day started this way and rightly so.

India was another route that we took frequently. One particular individual we took seven times to Delhi. He was a drugs dealer who entered the UK with impunity and was arrested each time he made it back onto the street. He did his sentence then deportation followed. (An Italian heroin smuggler and dealer equalled the seven times removed record).

During 1996, our office was visited by an Inland Revenue inspector; all of our computerized records were copied and examined. We were under investigation but the Revenue was playing their cards close to their chest. We had filed without fail our company's annual reports together with certified accounts. All was as it should be, I had no concerns whatsoever.

The Revenue was singing from a different hymn sheet, they wanted another meeting. This time I suggested our accountant should be in attendance. No way could I expect to have a clear understanding of tax law or the ways of the Inland Revenue. After all, don't we pay our accountants enough, so let's use their professional knowledge and expertise?

The meeting took place at the accountant's office. It was very clear the Revenue were not happy with the status of our medical security escorts. From day one I had insisted that all medical security escorts were contracted on a self-employed basis. My reasoning had not differed throughout our years of operation.

The longest working day I ever recorded was Fifty-four hours continued duty. That was a deportation to Fiji. Most operations entailed a working day of twenty-four hours. With such operational requirements, I could not see how we could meet the existing employment legislation. We could not meet the stated criteria set out within the act. It would be impossible to meet the working hour's restrictions that employed status dictates. The implications were such that our charges would need to be four times the level we were charging.

I took the decision to operate in the manner we did which seemed the only way available to us. The qualified escorts were paid a high hourly rate with all out of pocket expenses being reimbursed on a job to job basis. All bills submitted by the fifteenth of the month were paid by the first day of the following month by credit transfer, no waiting for cheques to clear.

Every escort was invited to perform their assignments; they all had the opportunity to say 'No'. My only stipulation was that the destination was not a choice option, for obvious reasons.

Self-employed status demanded such an arrangement.

Company debit cards were provided for hotel bills and fuel for company vehicles. The system worked well and the format was well tested. We kept meticulous records and monitored changes on a week to week basis. Whatever the destination, we were able to cost the mission to the nearest ten pounds.

The meeting with the Revenue was a shock to me, the attitude was almost hostile and amounted to a clear demand that either you change your operation to an employed status for the medical security escorts with immediate effect or we will sue you. Not only will we sue you, we will demand payment back for fourteen years to 1982 for unpaid national insurance for both employer and employee.

A 'fait accompli'; the Revenue inspector thought the job done.

I was not a happy bunny, this could wipe us out in one fell swoop and my gut feeling was someone has reported us to the Revenue, hence the investigation. Our accountant was sitting on the fence; he did not recommend a confrontation with the Revenue. Whilst he thought I was right, he suggested a change might be the prudent option. My opinion differed, I would contest the Revenue; I'm not a quitter.

For years I accepted, as most people do, that professionally qualified people must be right, they are the experts, so we pay for their expert advice. Oh how wrong I was, one big mistake, as time was to prove.

I was introduced to a chap called John Newth; in fact at one time we had lived next door to John's parents. John is the deputy editor of a monthly magazine called Taxation. He is a chartered accountant and an acknowledged expert on taxation law. A large, quietly spoken man, meticulous with details as you would expect. I was very impressed with our first meeting. Again our accountant was in attendance. I needed to be spot on with the information and back-up confirmation would not be out of place.

John Newth took the case on with some relish. He wanted copies of all my papers and time to consider the facts and would be in contact at a later stage. True to his word we did not have to wait, it wasn't long before John came back to me. He had prepared a report for the Inland Revenue in support of our operational position and he gave a number of stated cases in law in support of our argument.

The process was to last four years, yes four long years of argument, reports, reports upon reports; Tax Inspector, after Tax Inspector took us on. The threats continued: change or else. John did a great job and I could not have survived the ordeal without him. I would not have paid the Revenue because I couldn't, I did not have the money. I was emphatic that I was right any way. So, why on earth succumb to threats, in my mind the Revenue were demanding money with menaces. Either comply, do as we say or we will bankrupt you. What would you call it?

After four years we were summoned to attend yet another meeting at The Inland Revenue Office in London Road, St Leonards-on-Sea. John came with me. We were taken to an interview room; the Inland Revenue Inspector joined us carrying a huge file. He was accompanied by another man whom he introduced as an assistant. Untrue.

This gentleman was no assistant, he was the top Inland Revenue specialist investigator; John Newth knew him, he had attended a lecture given by this guy some two months previously.

John made a point of declaring the recognition; both faces twitched and flushed red. A little ruse had been blown. Now just threaten me again, buster, I thought.

We received official notice by way of a formal letter from the Inland Revenue that ASC could continue operating as we were. A four-year battle was over. Thank you John, without your support and determined effort I might not have been able to survive.

I often wonder just how many businesses and individuals go under in response to such threats from the Revenue when it is not justified. People do not have the will to mount a challenge with officialdom. It's obvious to me that these departments home in on the payers and pressurize in order to achieve the revenue targets that the departments are set by anonymous suits.

So it was business as usual.

Bob, a retired former Detective Inspector in Special Branch, accompanied me to the holding centre located at the Beehive at Gatwick Airport. The Beehive, so called because of its shape, and as I mentioned at the beginning, where I first started in business.

We were introduced to a guy that originated from St Vincent in the Windward Islands. He was being obstructive, not to put too fine a point on it. His immediate reaction to us was one of confrontation and intimidation, "I'm a US marine, none of you arse-holes are going to take me anywhere, I'll take you all apart." Well that said it all, didn't it, another day in paradise. Why change a habit of a life time? "Look mate. I don't know you from Adam. It's my job, with Bob here, to take you back to St Vincent via Barbados." He started interrupting "Shut your mouth for a minute and listen. We have two ways of dealing with these matters, the easy way or the hard way. The choice is yours. Just be assured that you are going home."

We put the cuffs on and made our way to the vehicle, then directly to the aircraft. Boarding was no problem. When seated in our normal location I could see the guy was crying. He turned to me and said, "I'm sorry about my attitude, they told me to act that way to avoid removal. Can we start over again?" "Hey, of course we can, I told you we had a choice of how to go, let's try the easy way." I said, and so it was to be. It turned out to be an interesting flight with plenty of conversation. Positioning to St Vincent required a further flight from Barbados on a small turbo prop aircraft operated by Liat (Leave Island Any Time). The very aptly named operation has no trouble living up to its name. No problem, it's the fantastic Caribbean, slow down and enjoy.

Arriving in the dark early evening having cleared arrivals, we stood outside the small terminal building and said goodbye and good luck. We went our separate ways, Bob and me in a taxi to the Tropic Breeze Hotel. Our friend went off in search of anybody he knew. St Vincent is that kind of place, a fantastic location betwixt the Atlantic and Caribbean and the Grenadines; an area of immense beauty. St Vincent drew the short straw; crime is rampant, poverty extreme. Corruption endemic, drugs being the major source of income. Fast, and I mean super fast, power-boats run drugs under the nose of the authorities. The Rasta farmers often protested outside the Government building when their ganja crop was burnt.

Piracy also occurs regularly within its waters. Targets are unsuspecting visiting mariners enjoying a sailing holiday in a fantastic location, frequently robbed and cast adrift. Not the ideal tourist-enticing description but there you go, this is life.

Gun crime is also a major problem and murders are commonplace. The death penalty still exists. The gallows are located at the prison on top of the hill at Fort Charlotte, overlooking Kingstown.

Barbados to the east, some eighty miles away. Bequia and Mustique and the Grenadines to the south and within view. The constant sound of reggae booms out from every vehicle, playing the drivers' preferred choice of music at full volume; it is almost a status symbol to be the loudest. The balmy evening with constant windward breeze makes a great atmosphere in which to sit on the veranda, partaking of a favourite liquid imbiber. Rum fits the bill and has a local flavour of its own.

The following morning Bob and I were sitting in an open dining area, with far-reaching views across the Bequia channel, having breakfast; it was about 08:00hrs and we were planning our day. I was facing the door and noticed a familiar face approaching. Our friend from the previous day came in with a broad smile on his face. "Hi Guys. Thought I'd track you down and show you around my home country. It's small but you'll need a guide. You were both great to me yesterday and I want to say thanks if that's OK". Bob and I exchanged glances, "Sounds a great idea to me. What do you say Bob?" "Why not, local knowledge we don't have, so why not" Our new friend's smile grew even broader.

The rest of the day turned out to be a complete education, one that I would not have missed for the world. We hired a vehicle and drove all over the island of St Vincent. With just forty-three miles of blacktop road it was not a marathon. We were shown the island from all angles, introduced to all his friends and relatives, both wives and all the kids, his mum and neighbours. The greeting that everyone uses is "Good night", it does not matter what the time of day is. This can be somewhat disconcerting but at least it raises a smile and that can't be bad. Smiles are plentiful in St Vincent. With the heavy accents and speed of delivery it can be difficult to understand what is said, but the longer you're exposed to speech, the easier it becomes. Your ears tune in and the brain picks it up.

Everyone knew who we were. The drugs baron and his henchman viewed us with suspicion, and I must admit that the hour we sat in the bar with them, I questioned my decision. It felt uncomfortable and I struggled to understand the purpose of this meeting. Was our man trying to make a point? I still don't know what that was about. The day was a great insight into the real manner in which a day is lived where survival is the only objective.

Back on the road our guide confirmed we had just met the number one man in the drugs business on the island. When you visit these islands and leave the tourist areas, and see how people live-no-the word should be survived. It opens your eyes. Your awareness becomes a far better qualified understanding.

The banana industry had been greatly damaged by EU import regulations. The sugar cane industry totally eliminated, likewise the historical arrowroot production.

Poverty is extreme but the people are rich in satisfaction, always a broad smile, the kids are clean and smart in school uniforms. Nobody goes hungry; the island is fertile, drop a seed and it will flourish. Captain Cook brought bread fruit to these islands and they flourish too.

Fruit grows in plenty, all manner of tropical varieties. No one goes hungry through poverty, everyone helps each other, whilst the soil provides. The community support displayed in St Vincent would be a prime example that could and should be emulated in the UK.

Cricket is played with fantastic enthusiasm wherever space permits, as you might expect. A volcanic island, the beaches are grey black sand, whereas Bequia, the closest island, has the beautiful white sand and palm tree-lined beaches, Princes Margaret Bay being a prime example. Both Bob and I scuba dive. The diving in St Vincent was superb. We both sail and sailing was and is fantastic. This place is on the edge of paradise in my book. I'll be back St Vincent, I've got a funny feeling we will meet again. Time will tell.

Bob and I returned to the UK, we had crammed a two-week vacation of activities into forty-eight hours; our man even came to see us off, his parting words. "If ever I'm deported again I'll ask for you two guys." We took that to be an endorsement.

A high profile removal was a young sixteen year old Nigerian. What was unique in this case was that the subject was to be taken to Guyana instead of Lagos. The destination had been arranged by the late Bernie Grant, MP. The Unison trade union was involved. Rodney Bickerstaff, the then General Secretary, took a high profile interest. The lad's mother was a nurse; his father had been removed to Lagos where, according to the publicity, his father had been killed. The fact that the second secretary from the British High

Commission in Lagos had visited the father in Lagos and found him to be alive and well had no relevance at all. The fact was just ignored.

Having collected the lad and his baggage from the detention unit at Harmondsworth, we met some relatives at Terminal Three who wanted to say goodbye. The relatives turned out to be a group of twenty-three protesters with the subject's sister. Whilst they were speaking to the lad through the window, my mobile phone rang. It was Rodney Bickerstaff, I recognized his voice. He asked me how the lad was and I gave him a heads up on the situation and he thanked me. I than called the visit to an end, amid shouts of protest. I was driving the vehicle and headed straight for our security gate.

Having cleared security, we met up with the duty CIO who had been detailed to observe the removal. As we approached the aircraft, which was located on a remote stand, away from the terminal, it was clear that a reception committee were waiting for us, press and TV cameras.

They were after the shot of this poor young kid being dragged up the aircraft steps yelling and kicking. We had time to spare so I asked the lad how he felt, did he want to speak with the media? I was totally surprised by his answer, "No way, these people have used my case to promote their cause without taking my feelings into consideration, they can go to hell." I suggested that we had an alternative. All the passengers were being bussed out to the plane, why not join the bus? "Great" he said "let's do it." I then said "Look they want us to be pictured taking you on the aircraft using force; you know what they're after don't you?" He said, "Well they're not getting it." The two escorts and the lad boarded the aircraft in line with the other passengers. Neither the press or the TV camera men recognized the lad.

They were somewhat pissed off when they were told he was already on board.

The CIO shook my hand and said, "Nice one Barry, you have no idea what grief this one has been." We watched the aircraft taxi off towards the departure runway. The lad returned to the UK within six months.

An Albanian national had been a subject which LPI had been tasked to remove but failed three times. I was called and asked to attend a meeting at Gatwick. The chap was a dirty protestor and described as violent and unstable. He had damaged five cells in the Scottish prison where he was currently staying. He had a habit of covering himself and his cell in faeces and shrieking at the top of his voice. "How do we remove this one?" was the HMI's question.

My suggestion was an air-ambulance, position to Edinburgh then direct to Tirana, a Lear 35 with a stretcher that would work. I priced the charter and obtained three quotes. If the Home Office had enquired, the price would have been five thousand pounds more. Two days later we were enroute to Edinburgh in the Lear jet, with three escorts and one driver. The minibus we hired at the airport. On arrival at the prison, the Governor, a short stocky dour Scot (why are they all dour Scots that I meet?) met us. I had difficulty cutting through his broad accent. What he was saying was "you've no chance with this one Jimmy. He's fighting crazy and covered in shit."

Being the eternal optimist, I commented on the weather and asked where we needed to go, an escort was provided to guide us around the blocks to the segregation unit.

With an expensive aircraft sitting waiting for us we had a job to do. We were taken straight into the segregation unit. Eight prison officers joined us; they were in full riot gear. I felt we were a tad under dressed. Three Perspex shields were produced. What's this all about? I asked "This is one bad bastard here; he's caused us one hell of a lot of grief" said a two- pip prison officer standing alongside me. The noise was as I described an endless shriek. Within four minutes we left the prison, five in number. Our man in a painter's suit with elasticated wristbands and ankles. The duty Governor was at the gate as we left, he beckoned me over. "That's one difficult individual, don't bring him back here." I think he said, I still struggled to understand him. The accent was so heavy. No reflection on my Scottish friends, but hell, give me a break, it isn't that easy if you're not tuned in. I half suspected the accent was tweaked up for my benefit just to take the piss out of these English guys. No doubt they had a bloody good laugh at our expense. So be it, the problem had been removed from their jurisdiction.

Back to Edinburgh Airport directly to the Lear jet awaiting us at the general aviation terminal. We were loaded and airborne within twenty minutes. Tony was left behind to return the minibus and then take a scheduled, flight back to Gatwick. All worked well until four hours later the Captain called me to the flight deck, a matter of eight feet ahead. "We can't find the bloody airport, visibility is getting bad, we may need to divert. Unless we see the runway in the next three minutes we need to divert to Athens. We have mountains all around and we are low on fuel. The airport closes at 15:00hrs, they don't have any lights. It was 14:40hrs. Suddenly, just about six miles ahead, a strip was glistening. Aircraft could be seen on the ground but no runway lights at all were visible. "What's that" both the first officer and I said in unison "Let's hope it is" said the pilot. We landed twelve minutes later. As soon as we stopped and the door was opened, I jumped out and ran to the rear of the aircraft.

I peed for England, I was bursting. The tension had got to me. Sorry to be so graphic but that's how it was.

Our passenger was unloaded, the aircraft was refuelled and we left as soon as we could.

I was forced to make contact with HM Customs and Excise and request a meeting at the VAT office.

The meeting was heated from my direction, I stressed that ASC was now in a situation where for the third quarter in succession, we had no choice, we were forced to pay a VAT quarterly return of a substantial sum to Customs and Excise of which not one penny had been received in payment from the Immigration Service, another department at the Home Office.

I would make this payment but it was the last, having paid over ninety thousand pounds under these circumstances enough was enough. My suggestion that Customs & Excise should walk along the corridor at the Home Office, collect the money from Immigration and send me what was left went down like a lead balloon.

The House of Commons at the time was pursuing legislation in respect of late payment interest which, once in law, provided a solution to some extent. It became law in November 1998 but was not retrospective.

I contacted the local Customs office VAT collection department located in Hastings and explained the scenario. I might just as well have talked to myself. One Home Office department will not communicate with another I was told. It's my problem, either pay the VAT or we will sue and even wind the company up. Demanding money with menaces crossed my mind. My priority was always to get the staff paid first, they had mortgages and families to feed, bills to pay. Without exception, they all responded to our duty calls so I had a clear duty to get them paid in a timely fashion which I did without fail.

That feeling of déjà vu, here we go again, yet another Government department that wants to put me out of business. Do we need this all over again?

My letter refusing to make any more payments did not go down well, even with what I thought was justification.

At this time, we lived in a rural location near Rye, in East Sussex a great spot at the top of a valley in an oast house. I had the office on tap so, whatever the time of day, we were up and running. We maintained 24 hour round-the- clock availability and that's what we provided. No half-cocked measures, we were what we purported to be.

This location provided an eight-year period in which it allowed us to pursue both social and sporting pursuits. I was fortunate enough to be able to ride frequently, participating in equestrian events with my 19h2" gelding Major Catastrophe and my 17h2" black mare Shenandoah. Both show jumping and three- day events. All far removed from my initial introduction to horses in London.

We were notified of yet another VAT officer's inspection, date and time set. The inspector arrived, a very nice lady who spent the day with us going through the books and computer records. Our book-keeper, Christy Boyd, had been with us for some years. Her system was first class and she was right on top of the situation. We broke off lunch-time and all sat around the kitchen table, had coffee and my wife prepared garlic mushrooms on toast, the smell wafted around the kitchen. I invited the VAT inspector to joins us, which she did. The smell of the mushrooms got to her, I think. We all chatted and enjoyed the lunch. It transpired the inspector's family were of Jamaican origin. Lunch over, and back to the inspection. As four o'clock in the afternoon approached the inspection was over. The telephone had not stopped ringing all day, that's how it was most days.

The Inspector's list contained five entries, questions which Christy was able to address by producing the filed documentation. The lady then suggested we should go on to a cash accounting system for paying due VAT, the company paying the VAT to Customs & Excise automatically as it's received from customers. That is the simple description of the cash accounting system. This could well be the solution that we needed to aid our cash flow. A great suggestion which merited consideration and implementation for ASC, it was just about three years nine months too late. Why had we never been offered this remedy nearly four years previously? At least five VAT inspections had been carried out at which times I had stressed our ongoing problem with the Home Office and our stressed cash flow.

Two years were devoted to attaining the ISO 9002 certification. Once attained, ASC would be the first certified company with the deportation classification; the approved protocol must then be implemented and adhered to. Regular checks are made to insure the system is maintained. The costs, without staff costs, amounted to over nine thousand pounds for us to complete the process. All operational manuals and the implemented system were in place. The final stage required an operational observation in order to monitor our procedures. This required three full days of monitoring to be carried out by an independent examiner.

I had to request permission for the final examination. My written request for the final authority was vetoed by the Immigration procurement unit. This made no sense at all to us. Whilst we were striving to demonstrate that our protocol was aimed at the highest level, our day to day practices were totally transparent. Furthermore, the qualification was a stipulated requirement for companies involved in deportation. What was going on?

It took another year before we saw any sign of LPI, as they liked to be known, the managing director was Tom Smith. He put himself about, bad mouthing us, describing us as or ASC as, "Rent a thug " and also proclaiming to be a former security service officer. Not a claim that is usually made if genuine. He collected company directorships like people collect recipes. To set up a company using a competitor's readily acknowledged identification sets a person apart, but to do it twice sets a pattern. Why set up a company called ASCL Ltd? Just what did he have for an agenda? We did not have to wait long to find out.

The latter end of 1996 produced a published notification in an EU publication of a request- for-tenders process to be held by the Home Office for the removal contract. Strict stipulations were stated for qualified companies to take part. ASC was one of eight companies which tendered in compliance with the rules. Strict submission dates were set and a decision date was confirmed. The date passed whilst we waited and waited and, yes, waited. The declaration date passed three times. What the hell am I talking about? How can a declaration date pass three times? Answer: when it's the Home Office. It took the procurement unit three years to declare that the tender process had been cancelled. Interim enquiries as to the status of the tender were just fielded by pathetic excuses. We were just placated in order to keep things ticking over. With the benefit of hindsight, the pattern was clear.

What they really meant was that the preferred company hadn't won, so why declare a preferred bid; let's wait until we can fix it so that they meet the criteria. Oh hush my mouth, that can't be so, can it? Stand by folks, read on.

A search of Company House records revealed that in fact LPI was insolvent in 1997, not the ideal status to warrant the award of a five-year contract one would think. So let's cancel the process for a while, sounds good to me. That will work. I can just hear the conversation taking place.

Our payments were now being made via the Paymaster General's office in Liverpool; at least payments would arrive in the bank almost on a daily basis. I sound as though I'm droning on, which I am of course, but that's how it was, a never ending spiral, not up but down. Into a large void.

The marked effect of late payment over a long period is the ultimate erosion of profit, in fact the profitability just evaporates. Other costs are incurred so the process is unavoidable.

In 1999 I entered the company into a voluntary arrangement with its one creditor, the Inland Revenue. Not a good move as it turned out. I pursued the same line with the revenue as I did with customs and excise it was the truth so why not.

I was summoned to Lunar House and the ninth floor which housed the top man the Director of enforcement, now Colin Harbin. He was without doubt somewhat vexed, the mood was clearly displayed. He threw his dummy out of the pram. Quibell ushered me into Harbin's office.

Harbin offered his hand and said, "I'm sorry we have never met after all this time, I've heard a great deal about you and your company. You have always completed the tasks we have set you in a first class manner. For which we are very grateful." we sat down, then he changed down a mood or two, and said "Why the hell didn't you tell us about this huge debt that hadn't been paid?" Harbin barked at me. I burst out laughing, reached into my case and produced a file of the past minutes of the debrief meetings spanning eight years. I said, " May I suggest you read these or better still ask the same question again but direct it to your Assistant Director standing next to you." "Well Paul?" Quibell said," It's been an ongoing problem; I thought we were on top of it. Barry we can't use a company that's in a CVA it gives us a problem." I said, "We have a speedy solution pay ASC and we can then pay the revenue." "It's not that simple we are well over budget." Quibell said. Harbin then said," We must get this sorted out without any further delay. Barry you should have picked up the phone and told me." My reply "Ok now it's all down to me that takes the biscuit!"

After all this time the clearer picture was emerging, they had been robbing peter to pay Paul. Playing games with their budget at our expense. The meeting was very brief I left under no illusion; I'd pissed the suits off big time.

A payment for seventy-five thousand pounds came through within a week; I guessed they must have had a whip round for us.

Work still came in, about 600 completed removals in 1999. Over 5000 removals in total and only nine complaints. That was a track record to be proud of when dealing with exceptional risk removals.

Well, what do you know, up pops the call for tenders yet again. This time October 1999 is the deadline for documents to be submitted.

After we attended a pre-tender briefing, it took us a month to complete our extensively detailed documentation. A great deal of work went into the preparation of the documentation; figures were calculated and double checked by our accountant.

Announcement date of the tender result was to be 20th December 1999. As with all deadline dates issued by IND

Procurement, they don't mean a thing unless they want them to.

On the 20th January 2000 at 11:25hrs a CIO Dennis Hassett phoned me from Lunar House. "Bad news. LPI have been awarded the contract. ASC came third, you didn't make the grade." "I'm not best pleased" I said. Dennis laughed and said;" I bet you're not." the phone went down.

Eighteen years of first hand experience, 5000 removals, just nine complaints and forty-three letters of commendation, "We didn't make the grade." Rubbish? Yes.

I later established that LPI had been told on 13th December that they were the preferred provider. From insolvent company to preferred provider within nine months, that was some formula for success. The CBI would covet this format; they would be interested in this miracle, no doubt.

Is that a whiff of rotting kippers in the air? The stench was stronger than Billingsgate on a hot summer's day.

I did another search on LPI just out of interest.

As I read the details, why was I not surprised? Colin Manchip CBE was now a director of LPI; the former Director of Immigration enforcement (none other) popped up, as can happen, as a director of a company insolvent the previous year, now with a seven million pounds contract. What a bloody coincidence. Wow...

To make matters even worse, Reliance Security were in second place, having been caught previously employing illegal immigrants, made not the slightest element of difference. Clearly it enhanced their position. The stated tender requirement of a proven track record in the field had been disregarded. No, wait a minute, perhaps employing illegals provides the qualification. Another coincidence, no doubt, of course, how could it be anything else? Double Wow...

Along with my PA and our solicitor we attended a debrief at Lunar House which I recorded, Paul Quibell, Harry Horseborough and Dennis Hassett gave us two and a half hours of excuses, 90% of which did not stack up. I rattled Hassett's cage during an exchange of views. He lost control briefly, which I found satisfying.

The onus for selection was put at the door of HMI Brian Davidson located at Harmondsworth detention management unit.

He was unable to attend the debrief. He was sadly missed. Like a hole in the head. This politically motivated individual, about four feet six inches in his Cuban heels, had the biggest chips on his shoulders. In fact if he had dropped the chips and stood on them he would have observed a better world. He was so anti private sector, he spat as he spoke. When ever I was unfortunate enough to have to speak with him he dripped resentment. We were earning more than him and he monitored the invoices. This fact was a constant problem for him. He was in day-to-day operational charge of the detention and transport contracts. I had been aware of the fact that he preferred LPI and met with their directors frequently. Two of Davidson's staff used to keep me informed of what was going on. I guess the writing had been on the wall for some time but I had not recognised the indications. Instead, I had concentrated my effort on doing the job. I had been warned of overheard conversations which were anti ASC. It had been my decision to let matters go. Besides, what action could have been taken? The warning was purely hearsay. Not that I didn't trust the source. I did but I also respected the fact that they needed to retain their employment status.

Let me make it very clear that in my life I have only ever encountered four people whom I did not like and felt very uncomfortable in their presence. Brian Davidson was one of the four. We had a mutual dislike for each other. It was instant on my part. I did not trust him one inch. It was a gut feeling and I'm unable to be more specific in the description. Something was not right.

We left and slept on it. Then we went over the tapes and notes, all was not well in Dingle Dell. ASC had been royally stuffed, and how.

I have a problem inasmuch that if I have a situation with someone, I'll give them one more chance. I'll take the crap once, but not twice. Is it a problem? Maybe I'm too tolerant.

I know it's always been my biggest weakness. I trust everyone until they let me down it's just the way I am. This point has been made to me in recent years.

We all trust professional people to act in our interest, whether it is a doctor, solicitor or accountant after all, we pay for their professional expertise, don't we? They must act in our interest. I naively believed it to be so, alas. It isn't always the way it works out, believe me. I've learnt to the contrary to my cost.

All of our vehicle and staff air-side passes had to be surrendered. I was informed that the poisoned dwarf Davidson had written to British Airports Authority instigating this action. As he had not sponsored us in the first place, I questioned his action. Just what was his motivation? Davidson wrote to BAA informing them that ASC no longer needed air-side access. I just could not believe it. BAA immediately acted on Davidson's information and withdrew our air-side passes for both Heathrow and Gatwick Airports.

This action effectively put us out of business. It was the final blow. We were unable to even carry out carrier liability removals.

I have no doubt whatsoever that this was planned. I'm able to produce letters which clearly stated our status but certain individuals revoked that position in retaliation. This action cost us our house and business within two years.

It took me another month to compile all the documents I needed and I took the lot, with my very good friend and solicitor, Mark Culbert, to a pre-arranged meeting with Mr.Charles Wardle MP for Bexhill and Battle, my local MP.

Mark Culbert did a first class job presenting all the facts and figures, supporting the complex issues that we needed to highlight. Rarely in business do we encounter people whom you can also call friends. Mark is one of those exceptions.

Mr. Wardle took a while to read through the mound of papers. They were all in sequence, and cross indexed. He raised a few questions at a second meeting at his office in Bexhill, he wanted to take the matters to the Immigration Minister. He had already made an application for an adjournment debate in the House of Commons. The manner in which such debates are granted is by way of a lottery. His initial application was successful and a date was allocated. 24th May 2000.

I remain convinced that Mr. Wardle MP felt in total agreement with our conclusions that the tendering process had not been conducted within the rules laid down for procurement.

He presented our side in the debate with eloquence and expert delivery; eighteen points were made. The Home Office Minister, Barbara Roche MP, countered with agreement to review the position. Not really accepting any points until proven, which I fully understood. The matter was investigated; sixteen of the eighteen points were found to be questionable. I made a statement under caution: some seventy-two pages. The Metropolitan Fraud Squad was called in to investigate the matter in its entity. Not all of the witnesses were interviewed. The directors of LPI were not interviewed for a start. The fact that they had set up a company called ASC Ltd and had been purporting to be ASC for some time, which was a fraudulent activity, did not warrant investigation. Some Home Office investigation!

On behalf of Airline Security Consultants Ltd, I commenced legal proceedings against the Home Office Immigration department. Writs served, a response could not be avoided. After the exchange of a series of letters, the Home Office made an offer to settle out of Court which I accepted. Perhaps that had been a mistake, all of these issues needed to be brought out into the public arena. There again, we just wanted to move on.

Escorts are still being injured on a regular basis today. The conditions they fly under these days are dangerous. Sixty hours in economy, Heathrow to Fiji, four hours stop over, then return is bloody crazy. What do they need before they understand the first fatality?

There again it's the Home Office. "Not fit for purpose." Yes Minister, you're spot on. You're the only one with the balls to say so. What happens next, Minister?

Hire another group of consultants to tell them how to do the job? If I had the time I would take a very close look at these over-used so called consultancy companies themselves. Senior civil servants take early retirement then join such organizations as consultants. Hence we have a farce that develops. When in the job they needed to call on consultants to advise on policy and suitability of equipment, once out of the job they qualify as consultants. Why do I not understand what's going on? There again perhaps I do.

That appears to be the format or am I just being facetious? Not at all, it's happening all the time. Not just at the Home Office either.

The Hansard report 24/5/2000 on the adjournment debate, follows.

For the sake of complete accuracy I have sought and obtained permission to use the full text of the Hansard Record of the adjournment debate.

Parliamentary Licence   P2006000398

24 May 2000: Column 256WH

Illegal Immigrants

12.59 pm

Mr. Charles Wardle (Bexhill and Battle): I am grateful for the opportunity to draw attention to what appear to be serious irregularities on the part of the immigration service in the way in which the renewal of the contract for the escort of persons to be removed from the United Kingdom under the Immigration Act 1971 was conducted. I shall also refer to allegations of unacceptably late payments by the IS of money requested in invoices, involving delays of up to four years. I shall cite evidence of administrative chaos, and the failure of the IS to keep records of removals.

These matters were drawn to my attention by Mr. Barry Southon, who lives at Broadoak, Brede, in my constituency. He is the proprietor of Airline Security Consultants Ltd. ASC has worked for the IS for some 18 years. In this debate, I shall rely on what Mr. Southon has told me and shown me, which I take to be entirely sound.

At the outset, I should declare a past interest. I served as an Immigration Minister in the Home Office during the previous Parliament. I did not meet Mr. Southon in that capacity, however; I first encountered him when he came to one of my constituency advice surgeries in February this year.

I have the highest regard for the hard work and dedication shown by men and women in the IS, who must frequently operate in trying conditions. If, on some occasions in the past, I have expressed reservations about the management calibre of some senior officials in the immigration and nationality directorate, as it now is, that does not detract from my esteem for the achievements of rank-and-file members of the IS. However, none of that prevents me from putting the spotlight on what appears to show carelessness and malpractice on the part of a very few officials during the tender for the new escort contract.

I hope that, following this debate, the points that I raise will be investigated more closely, not only by the Minister-- to whom I have already written--but by the National Audit Office. I asked the Comptroller and Auditor General for a copy of the Public Services Contract Regulations 1993 in connection with the debate, and I intend in due course to draw to his attention what I have said today.

Mr. Southon tells me that, since he began working under contract to the IS in 1982, he has been personally involved in the escorted removal of more than 4,000 people from the UK. I am not aware of any significant criticism by the IS of the way in which ASC has operated during that period; indeed, I have been told that, in 18 years, only nine complaints have been made about ASC, all of which proved on further investigation to be without foundation. In contrast, I have seen copies of many commendations of ASC, from the Under-Secretary of State for the Home Department, the hon. Member for North Warwickshire (Mr. O'Brien), directors, an inspector, training teams, chief immigration officers and immigration officers. All have praised the company. Some of the most recent letters of commendation have expressed downright surprise that such an experienced team should be dropped at the very time when the British public looks to the IS to increase its effectiveness in removing immigration offenders.

24 May 2000: Column 257WH

Over the years since 1982, ASC has developed a highly efficient service in which security and medical escorts have been made available at just two hours' notice, together with a secure vehicle with airside access when required. Until 1994, it was the sole provider of escorted removals to the IS, but, following a written question tabled in 1994 by the Minister of State, Home Office, the hon. Member for Hornsey and Wood Green (Mrs. Roche), who will reply to the debate--she was then an Opposition Member, and I was the Minister--a second escort company, Loss Prevention International, was taken on at the instigation of a procurement official, Mr. Paul Quibell. From then on, ASC handled about 80 per cent. of the work and LPI about 20 per cent.

In 1996, ASC--presumably along with LPI--participated in a tender for renewal of the escort service contract, but, for some unexplained reason, that tender competition was never completed. It was eventually abandoned three years later, in July 1999. At that juncture, ASC was asked to re-tender, which it did, by submitting an 83-page document by the due date of 9 November last year. The result of the new tender was to be announced on 20 December, although, in fact, no such announcement was made on that date.

Only one of the companies that tendered in November was called in for a clarification meeting with the IS. That was the eventual winner, LPI, whose representatives met Mr. Hassett and other officials in Croydon on 13 December when, it is alleged, they were told that they had been successful. That was a week before the designated date for the announcement of the winner.

On 20 January, a month after the date on which the result of the tender process should have been announced, Mr. Hassett spoke to Mr. Southon on the telephone and confirmed that the contract had indeed been awarded to LPI. Mr. Hassett said that another bidder, Reliance, had been placed second, ahead of ASC. A meeting was arranged for 26 January, at which Mr. Quibell gave his reasons why ASC's tender offer had not succeeded. He said that ASC had, in particular, fallen short on standards of quality and training.

At the meeting, Mr. Quibell denied that LPI had been told on 13 December that it had won the contract, but, in his letter of 21 February to Mr. Southon's solicitor, he appears to have changed his position. In that letter, Mr. Quibell admitted that we had already . . . selected LPI as the contractor we proposed to appoint prior to calling the company in for . . . further discussion . . . LPI attended a meeting with us on 13 December to clarify a number of points . . . in order to allow us to proceed to award the contract.

In that letter, Mr. Quibell said that the successful tender offer by LPI and the second-placed tendered, Reliance, had set out a much more extensive package of training and a more comprehensive management structure. He said that the quality of systems and procedures offered by both those companies were supported by current accreditation to ISO 9002. What he did not say was that LPI's and Reliance's ISO 9002 accreditation was for activities other than deportations. The only company working for full accreditation for deportation is ASC, and the only reason for a delay in ASC's accreditation for that task is that the Home Office has refused to give the accreditation body permission to

24 May 2000: Column 258WH

Observe a removal by ASC. That was confirmed when I saw a fax from National Quality Assurance Ltd.'s regional office in London saying precisely that.

Mr. Quibell's allegation that ASC fell short of its competitors' training standards is, to say the least, strange. On 26 January, Messrs Quibell and Hassett claimed that ASC had afforded only a six-day training course, with no monitoring of staff or acceptance testing. They could not have read ASC's tender document very carefully. That document makes it clear on page 9 that the initial six days of induction training will be followed by operational training, to be conducted by experienced staff and recognised outside instructors. Pages 12 and 13 outline no fewer than 28 aspects of the on-going training sessions, and make it clear that great emphasis will be placed on training on the job. ASC should know how to train better than anyone else, as it is the only company with a sustained track record in the business.

Pages 41 and 43 of ASC's tender document show what training is to follow the induction course. Pages 23 and 45 describe performance monitoring, and the on-going assessment of escorts; pages 32, 49 and 50 explain how staffing levels will be adjusted to cope with the expected increase in the volume of work. Mr. Quibell and his colleagues were entirely wrong to suggest that the ASC tender document had nothing to say on that point.

Equally wrong was the assertion by the IS that ASC had failed to ensure that escorts would identify themselves properly. Pages 36 and 50 make clear precisely how escorts are to do that. Equally inaccurate was the IS's suggestion that ASC had ignored questions of quality and the issue of Investors in People. ASC's quality policy and the commitment to Investors in People is set out on page 5 of the tender document; similarly, page 11 sets out in detail ASC's security plan, and page 61, together with the letter at appendix 5, confirms that ASC has the ability to increase its insurance cover.

For all those reasons, the objections to ASC wheeled out by the IS simply do not stack up. Even if we assume for the sake of argument that LPI and Reliance had demonstrated a greater thoroughness than ASC in their plans, it is not good enough for the IS to claim that ASC did not have a detailed plan in its tender document when it certainly had precisely that.

As I have said, I wrote to the Minister earlier this month. I imagine that she has by now been able to compare the three tender documents from LPI, Reliance and ASC in the unamended form in which they were presented on or before 9 November last year. I hope that she will agree that it would be appropriate now for the NAO to examine those three documents, too. As I have said, it is something that I shall ask the CAG to do.

If the discrepancy between IS officials' criticism of ASC's tender document and the reality of what that document contains is not serious enough, there are other warning signals from the tender, about which the Chamber should be aware. The first concerns Reliance, which was placed second in the tender process. In 1995, the IS raided the offices of Reliance and found that no fewer than 15 of its employees were illegal immigrants. The Minister will, I hope, be able to explain why, under those circumstances, Reliance was placed second.

24 May 2000: Column 259WH

As for LPI, IS officials will no doubt have alerted the Minister to the controversy in which that company became embroiled over stowaways on a Nigerian-flagged vessel in Lagos harbour some years ago. Equally, I feel confident that she will have been informed of the occasion a few years ago when LPI used four escorts for a removal to Sierra Leone. The immigration offender being removed was put under sedation by LPI and was delivered unconscious at Freetown. None of LPI's four escorts on that case was medically qualified. All four were detained in Freetown for a week for questioning.

I have no doubt that the Home Office will have on its files the latest accounts for LPI and will be aware that, as recently as the 1997 financial year, it appeared to be insolvent. When the Minister replies, I hope that she will be able to assure the Chamber that she has examined its latest accounts and can confirm a substantial increase in capital since the end of that financial year.

ASC is not insolvent. I am assured that it has never traded while insolvent, although no thanks for that are due to the Home Office, which has an appalling record of delays in payments and non-payments of invoices due to ASC.

In the past, ASC regularly had monthly meetings in Croydon. Almost every time, the issue at the top of the agenda was slow payment. Some of the invoices have been outstanding for four years before payment has been made. The delays have had nothing to do with queries on the content of those invoices. At one time, the debt owed by the Home Office to ASC was about £250,000.

In 1997, ASC was not paid anything for four months because of a Paymaster General dispute in Liverpool, yet, at the same time, it paid more than £90,000 in VAT on invoices for which it had not received a penny from the Home Office. Repeated requests to the IS did not result in payment.

ASC claims, for example, that, if it had been able to charge interest on late payment from the Home Office prior to November 1988 in the manner subsequently required by legislation, it would have been able to claim an extra £400,000. That is the extent of the inefficiency and muddle over finances into which the Home Office appears to have got itself over a period of years. I hope that that has been remedied.

There has been an equally unsatisfactory muddle over records that the IS is supposed to have maintained concerning the removal of immigration offenders. Mr. Southon has assured me that, whenever Members tabled questions about the number of people removed, the IS had to seek urgent answers from ASC because there were no in-house records of its own on which it could rely.

I turn to a particularly disturbing facet of the run-up to the tender offer. I am told that an LPI director, whose name I can provide to both the Minister and, if I am asked to do so, the NAO, regularly entertained IS staff at Harmondsworth. I have been given the names of the IS staff who were entertained and offered other inducements. I am assured that ASC is willing to provide an affidavit to support that allegation.

24 May 2000: Column 260WH

The IS officials who were entertained told ASC that they were looked after by LPI and asked whether ASC was willing to do the same. Specifically, they asked whether ASC would "weigh in too." Mr. Southon tells me that he refused point blank, but after he did so the work placed with ASC from Harmondsworth declined noticeably. I am unwilling--I am sure that the Minister will agree with this--to name in the Chamber officials who are the subject of those allegations, but I shall provide their names to the Minister and to the NAO if required to do so.

I have been alerted to reports that a former senior enforcement official at the IS has joined the board of LPI, since when that company appears to have gained favour, despite its modest track record and past inadequate capitalisation. I worked with that individual when I was at the Home Office and had no complaints about him. Nevertheless, it is said on the Home Office grapevine and among reputable home affairs press correspondents that, following that person's retirement, he secured for himself an unusual assignment in Russia, where, it is said, he produced a highly original guidance manual for clients about ways in which they might obtain entry into the UK with the minimum difficulty.

Two experienced journalists have related that story to me over the past year, but I did not feel that there was sufficient hard evidence from what I was told to raise the matter with Ministers then. In view of that official's involvement with LPI now, and LPI's success in the tender offer in the face of an apparent shut-out of so much of the ASC tender document, all those things now must surely merit closer investigation.

I have been informed that, on 2 March, at a meeting in Dover, the director of the immigration and nationality directorate, Ms Collins, was asked why the contract had been awarded to LPI instead of ASC. I understand that she seemed unaware that LPI had obtained the contract. That was more than two and a half months after LPI had been told of its success and a month and a half after ASC had been informed that it had lost out. I remind the Chamber of my past criticism of management performance among senior officials at the Home Office. That seems to be yet another clear example of an abysmal lack of communications.

I point out a frustrating catch-22 situation in which ASC has been placed following its failure to secure the contract. Mr. Quibell has told Mr. Southon that, where a carrier-- for example, an airline or ferry company--brings an illegal immigrant into the UK, that carrier is now responsible for the removal of that immigration offender. Historically, the IS has arranged for the deportation and then invoiced the carrier for the costs. Mr. Quibell has said to Mr. Southon that, as from April this year, under new legislation, carriers have had to contract directly with escort companies for the removal of those offenders. Mr. Quibell went on to say that, although the main IS contract had been awarded to LPI, he hoped that ASC would still carry out carriers liability removals under the new arrangements. To be able to provide that service to the carriers, ASC needs sponsorship from the IS to obtain airside passes, but Mr. Quibell has said that IS sponsorship of such airside clearance can no longer be made available. Thus, with that catch-22 situation, ASC finds that insult has been added to injury.

24 May 2000: Column 261WH

Under all those circumstances, I hope that the Minister will review as a matter of urgency the conduct of the tender procedure. I am sure that she will appreciate how important it is that ASC and the wider public receive an explanation of why there appear to be so many anomalies between what IS officials said on 26 January, what Mr. Quibell wrote in his letter of 21 February and the reality of the content of the ASC tender document.

1.18 pm

The Minister of State, Home Office (Mrs. Barbara Roche): I am grateful to the hon. Member for Bexhill and Battle (Mr. Wardle) for providing me with an opportunity to set the record straight about the award of the overseas escorting contract. I remember when I was in opposition asking a number of questions and taking an interest in that area of work. We now find ourselves in different roles on the subject.

It may be helpful if I say why it is necessary for us to escort some people overseas and why it was necessary to retender the contract. The immigration service and the immigration and nationality directorate remove about 39,000 people per year from the United Kingdom. Most people who are directed to leave accept that they must do so, but a small minority--around 600--must be escorted to ensure that they reach their destination. The majority of those escorts are for security reasons.

For more than six years, the overseas escort service has been provided by two suppliers: Airline Security Consultants and Loss Prevention International. ASC has provided the service for considerably longer than LPI, as the hon. Gentleman said. Owing to the new regulations specified in the Immigration and Asylum Act 1999, it will be necessary for escorting staff to be certified as fit and proper persons to conduct escorts under the arrangements set out in the Act. Existing contracts did not provide a satisfactory platform to achieve that; nor was it possible to demonstrate that the Home Office was getting best value for money or proper continuity of service by using those arrangements.

Consequently, and following an investigation and recommendation by the National Audit Office, it was decided to hold a competition last year for the provision of an overseas escorting service by one contractor. That was done on the basis of what the NAO had to say. Both ASC and LPI, which had previously been providing escort services, were aware that that would happen, and they participated in the competition.

The hon. Gentleman has made some allegations about LPI. I understand from the brief advice that I have taken that, at this stage, we have no knowledge of these accusations.

However, I shall investigate his allegations and write to him.

The competition was run in accordance with the Public Services Contract Regulations 1993, using the restricted procedure. The contract was initially advertised in the Official Journal of the European Communities and also in Government Opportunities. As a result of the advertisement, eight companies were invited to submit tenders, although two of these subsequently withdrew from the competition. Of the six remaining tenders, LPI's was judged to be the best, in that it offered the most economically advantage

24 May 2000: Column 262WH

Proposal with both the best technical solution and best overall value for money to the taxpayer.

The hon. Gentleman mentioned the sequence of events. Although it was hoped to announce the results of the tender on 20 December 1999, there were a number of practical issues to be resolved before the contract could be signed. These included confirmation that the insurance meeting our full requirements was in place. All matters were resolved and a decision was finally taken and notified to tenderers in writing on 17 January 2000. The contract was finally signed on 8 March. As the hon. Gentleman knows from his past experience and from his present position in the House, such decisions are taken by officials and Ministers are informed. I wish to make it clear that I had no part in the decision-making process.

The hon. Gentleman has suggested that the competition for the contract was not handled properly. I shall carefully examine his remarks when they appear in Hansard tomorrow. I can say only that, from the information that is before me, the procedures were fully complied with under the Public Services Contract Regulations 1993. The competition also had independent oversight from the Home Office procurement unit and the Treasury Solicitor, and both are completely satisfied with the process. That is important because those bodies are in place to make checks and balances. The hon. Gentleman will know that all our procurement procedures are subject to audit.

The hon. Gentleman has mentioned, as has ASC, that the company does not believe that the tender documents were properly scrutinised. There was the example of staff training. I am advised that the training proposals submitted by ASC with the tender were inadequate. It was only at a subsequent meeting on 26 January 2000 that ASC suggested that the training proposals were only indicative and represented one week of a programme of several weeks. It was alleged by ASC that the tender had not been read properly, but it was unable to show in its documentation any details about the further expansion of the one-week example into a full programme.

Mr. Wardle: I am acutely aware that I have taken more than my share of time, but may I say that I fully understand that the Minister was not involved in the procedure? I hope that she will find time to study the contracts, because that is what I shall be asking the Comptroller and Auditor General to do as well. I have no idea whether he will do that, but it would be a great help if the hon. Lady were to examine them.

Mrs. Roche: I shall examine what the hon. Gentleman has said when his remarks appear in the record.

The evaluation process cannot be expected to take account of things which might or might not be intended. It can take account only of the contents of the documentation.

The hon. Gentleman has raised extremely serious matters, and I want to deal with them in the time that is available to me. He implies that there has been some misconduct in the relationship between IND officials and ASC and LPI. Similar implications were contained in a letter from ASC's solicitors dated 7 March, in which

24 May 2000: Column 263WH

It is alleged that two members of staff had been socialising with LPI directors. I take such allegations extremely seriously. The two members of staff concerned deny the implications absolutely.

We asked the solicitors to provide specific details so that the matter could be investigated. To date, more than two months later, they have not done so, and I take great exception to that. If the hon. Gentleman is able to provide specific examples, I will ensure that there is an investigation. As I have said, these are serious allegations.

Mention has been made of a retired director of the immigration service. Again, serious allegations were made by the hon. Gentleman. I am informed that the retired director's appointment had no direct bearing on the decision to award LPI the contract. He did not attend any of the meetings with LPI and made no contact with officials responsible for the procurement process. As I have said, it was run under the 1993 regulations.

The hon. Gentleman made other allegations, which I heard for the first time. He repeated gossip. These are serious matters to raise on what is effectively the Floor of the House. As he is entitled to do, he raised them with the protection of privilege. I will consider the allegations. If he has any evidence to show, I will ensure that a proper investigation is conducted.

The hon. Gentleman mentioned late payment and the relevant legislation. I am responsible for it because I campaigned for its introduction when in opposition. It was one of the measures that I took through the House when I had the privilege to be a Department of Trade and Industry Minister. The hon. Gentleman will recall that I was critical of late payment by government, and made it a feature of what I was doing in opposition. I have in mind particularly the record of the previous Government, of whom the hon. Gentleman was a member. I am assured that payment practices, which were not good in the past, have improved dramatically. That is important.

It is important also for us to place arrangements for escorting people away from the United Kingdom on a better contractual basis. That is what we have sought to do. The hon. Gentleman mentioned the knowledge of senior management in terms of the contract. It was known at senior levels of management that the contract had been placed. The hon. Gentleman suggested that, in regard to accreditation, ASC was placed in not as good a position as the other companies. That is certainly not the case. On the basis of the information that I have seen, I can reassure the hon. Gentleman and the House on that point.

Given what I have seen so far and what has been presented to me--it was seen by the relevant bodies, including the Treasury--everything was done to meet the bona fides of the process. I shall carefully examine the record to ascertain what was said. I shall write to the hon. Gentleman as soon as possible. However, it is incumbent on him and on those who have provided him with information to provide that information, rather than merely making allegations--

Mr. Barry Jones (in the Chair): Order. Time is up.

Thirty-six people contracted to Air Line Security Consultants Ltd needed to find an alternative source of income with effect from 1st April 2000, yes a significant date.

The post was full of letters for the next month or so from CIOs, IOs and HMIs as word filtered around that we were out. We all really appreciated their comments and the fact that they had taken the time and effort to say farewell. That meant a great deal to me and the team. These were people at the sharp end who knew what goes on and the difficult environment in which we functioned.

I needed a new direction once again. Both of our daughters by now had left home and had families of their own. The phone stopped ringing. That was a major readjustment for me and it took some getting used to. I would go to the phone; lift the receiver to make sure the line was ok. The switch off or down turn, whatever you want to call it, was difficult for me to accept after eighteen years of pressure on which I had thrived (my opinion only) others would disagree. My wife was pleased with the break; we could now pursue a social life for a change.

Dover was taking a pounding with a vast daily increase in people-smuggling, so we had a few days out doing a recce.

I went to Mexico and Guatemala with an American contact of mine. I wanted to see how the Mexican authorities dealt with their border controls and vehicle examination in particular.

This was a great exercise and I gathered a huge amount of data from eight hectic locations. X-ray equipment was in use and was a substantial deterrent. Large quantities of drugs and people smuggling, were being detected using this technology, although the vehicles were not being operated within their safety envelope. Which I found surprising. When in Rome do as the Romans do, came to mind.

Within two weeks I attended a meeting in Paris with the ITRHA (International Road Hauliers Association) they indicated that they were very interested in my developing project and wanted to act quickly in order to provide their members with a vehicle search facility immediately prior to boarding the ferry or tunnel transit.

The x-ray search process was a five minute process and could be performed by passing down a line of queuing vehicles. The time factor was, I thought, questionable because it would depend upon the level of expertise demonstrated by the operator. Each search vehicle cost some two million pounds, and then you had the operating costs. My project required four of these vehicles, of which three would operate for 24 hours, seven days a week. The fourth vehicle being a backup service replacement used to ensure the operational flow.

The project had the potential to save United Kingdom Ltd one hundred and seventy million pounds per year. The security screening system would have been a major deterrent to people smugglers.

I'm totally aware that sophisticated counter measures can be taken but they can also be spotted. Time was to our advantage if only agreement could be reached.

I had already consulted a French attorney and a framework document had been drafted. I knew the criteria which UK immigration wanted to achieve on the other side of the Channel. I set up a meeting in Calais with the Port Authority and the ferry operators, all were people whom I had encountered through the years with the exception of the Truck Operators association. I did a presentation using the Mexican scenario as an example. Interest was there without a doubt but funding was the big question. Who should pay a British problem, not ours, was the French stance. If the British didn't offer such incentives, they would not be queuing to get in, was the French argument in a nutshell.

The ferry operators were being fined two thousand pounds a time for each illegal found on board on arrival in Dover. Also fined were the truck drivers, who were also hit hard by these crippling fines. If the port would agree, I had a source for the equipment available; we would need a contract with either the ferry operators or the French port operators. The maths worked out, it could be a viable business.

P&O were keen; Sea France operational staff were keen but "NON" came the word from Paris. X-ray is not acceptable, it might be dangerous was the feeble excuse. We had already cleared this factor with the Ministry, the radiation levels were less than a domestic micro-wave oven. The French were adamant it would not happen.

My solution hadn't been far off target because the Home Office purchased one of the x-ray vehicles for Customs and Excise. I had been summoned to Customs & Excise HQ, they wanted to know why I was so interested in these vehicles.

It would have been futile to pursue the French to change their mind; it was political and they were entrenched in the position they were taking.

Not being a quitter can be expensive, as I would discover. Back to the drawing board and back to the USA. They had equipment which might well fit the requirement. Heart Beat Detectors, this was state-of-the-art technology, already tried and tested in protected environments (this is highly significant) and used at US prisons and nuclear power stations to search vehicles moving in and out. The proven worth had been established, escapes had been thwarted. The big plus, no radiation at all. This new system was not x-ray.

I visited Houston, Texas and met with the Corporation owner, Mark White, a larger-than- life character, a former Democratic Governor of Texas. You can't help but like the guy, we got on well and he was very responsive to my proposition. He wanted to sell the HBD units and Europe was untapped. So he told me. Not quite the true position with all these deals. Greed promotes manipulation of the truth. The equipment was already in the hands of an agent, but they had only sold a few units.

I wanted one unit on loan for three months to enable trials to be run so that the system could be evaluated. "No problem, Barry, you've got it, just tell us where and when." Well that was a promising start. I set up an agreement with P&O to provide the equipment on a three- month trial to assess equipment on site. I made it abundantly clear that this equipment works well in a protected environment; out of the wind it takes forty seconds to check a lorry once the driver has switched off and left the cab. The plan was to provide a long shelter which all trucks would pass through. The trucks, once cleared, would pass through to a sterile zone prior to boarding the ferry. Any suspect vehicles would be escorted to a secondary examination area.

The equipment could be operated by two trained staff, three during peak times; forty to fifty vehicles could be processed per hour, per operational system. Six HBD systems, strategically placed, could cope with Calais traffic.

Ferry schedules must be protected, so speedy, accurate examination was the key. P&O undertook to set up an examination shed at a pre-arranged location in a suitable zone which I had been shown and dates were agreed. Four people from Houston arrived with the equipment and I met them at Ashford. We all made our way to Calais and checked into the Tulip Hotel. We were scheduled to meet with P&O at 08:00hrs the next day. All went well at the initial meeting. The formal introductions completed, the equipment was demonstrated in the conference room. After lunch we were to move to the examination shed. I could not see the examination shed at the location I'd been shown a month earlier by the P&O manager, which was a concern to me. Our hosts explained that the Port Authority had vetoed the original location and had insisted on another location. When we saw the location, the Americans went into panic mode. The shed had been erected alongside a berth, the ground vibrated in time with the ferry's generators. This was crazy; this was a deliberate attempt to sabotage the trials.

The Americans worked for twenty-four hours trying to eliminate the local environmental problems but it was driving the software crazy. The system was working to accuracy capacity of merely 33%; we needed to be 1500 feet south of this location. In fact, we tried the equipment further south and it registered as 100% effective.

Senior immigration personnel visited us, along with P&O senior staff, and we explained the difficulties with this changed location. Still, the demonstration was completed, the software provided vehicle records and photo evidence but the environment was an obstacle we had not bargained for. The licensed suppliers were not prepared to leave their equipment for the prearranged period, which was understandable.

I submitted a draft proposal to HM Immigration via the Home Secretary. In fact, it took three submissions before we received a reply which told us to get lost effectually. I guess my name was guaranteed to ensure rejection.

There we go again, we had given it a try, and it wasn't to be. Or was it?

My wife and I took a six-month break; it was well past time and a badly needed period of R&R. We headed off to the Caribbean, no prizes for guessing where.

St Vincent and the Grenadines beckoned us.

During a prolonged stay you can discover a great deal about a country and its people. Post 9/11 the area was suffering from the lack of tourist dollars. In common with many other such areas.

From previous visits, I had established two needs St Vincent had. Cricket was, as expected, the number one game. I had managed to lay my hands on a substantial amount of used cricket equipment. Hampshire CC was magnificent in providing items. Every bit of equipment was received with grateful thanks and distributed by the local Rotary Club. Also, I still had four air-craft litters (stretchers) which were needed desperately in order to set up an air-ambulance service and they were put to good use.

We rented an apartment from the resident surgeon, a Cuban with whom I'm pleased to say we became good friends. Basic but all we needed. The veranda had a view to the west and provided a great location for sun-downers and spectacular sunsets. The advantage of a swimming pool was not lost either, we used it daily. The garden provided an assortment of fruit which we picked as required.

Plenty of sailing resulted and there was ample time to explore all of the Grenadine Islands, a true bonus of which we took full advantage.

Just prior to Christmas, my younger brother Malcolm telephoned me. He had been diagnosed with an inoperable brain tumour. We were all devastated. We returned home. I needed to spend time with Malcolm. He had a sailing boat which was moored on buoys in the Medway. Malcolm wanted a day on the boat; that day was special for both of us.

When diagnosed Malcolm was given six months; he lost the battle five months later. Never once did he ask "Why me?" He was a magnificent example to us all. Over two hundred people attended his funeral. It's now four years and the void still exists. That will never change.

"OH WHAT A MESS"
"OH WHAT AN UNDERSTATEMENT"

Back in the UK, after almost a year, it was time to relocate. I was both pleased and surprised to be contacted by a senior Immigration officer based near Heathrow. She wanted a meeting as soon as possible; she needed to speak with me as a matter of some urgency.

After the informal exchange of greetings and a quick catch up we got down to the nitty-gritty.

It seems that during my absence, the Immigration service procurement unit, none other, had contracted to purchase twenty-six Avian heartbeat detector systems through the UK agent ISL Intelligent Security Limited. The contract price was in the region of a half million pounds. A very nice deal, and discounted as you would expect. The equipment warranted a full maintenance service contract which cost the Immigration Service twelve thousand pounds a month yes £12000 each month.

She wanted to know if I still had any involvement with Geovox in Houston Texas. I indicated that I could go direct to the President of company. It was not a problem for me.

A serious problem had occurred during the period of the contract outlined above.

Only fourteen of the Avian units had been delivered out of the twenty-six ordered and paid for. Not only that, sixty thousand pounds had been over-invoiced and paid in error. A large number of spare parts had been ordered and invoiced, taking the budget through the roof. The IND had screwed up big time. Promises of repayment from ISL had not materialized; the Audit Commission were about to descend.

What do you think can be done?

If I were in your position, the first thing I would do is get straight on to ISL by phone, demand the immediate delivery of the remaining units within the next twenty-four hours.

Insist delivery is made to a precise location by a set time. Confirm the conversation with a fax. Then just wait and see what happens.

Furthermore, the repayment of the overpaid sums must be demanded in writing immediately, set a time limitation. Whatever you do, don't leave it in the pending tray.

I know the company and I suspect they will not be able to deliver the complete items in the stated time frame. My suspicion is you've been taken for mugs. I'd even put money on a wager that you have been buying your own units as spares.

"Oh what a mess." she said. I said "Look, keep me posted on the response. I would imagine the units are not going to be complete, you'll need to give me a precise list of what's missing. I'll see what can be done." I left and returned home, thinking once again what goes around comes around. I could not believe that the actions I had mentioned had not already been pursued, of course they must have been. Probably a number of times but what was clear: the desired response had not been achieved. Why contact me? I again assumed that desperation was setting in and self- preservation was the order of the day. The shit was about to hit the fan.

Two days later another phone call, "You were spot on. The units are incomplete and one system is missing altogether. Even the leads and sensors are missing." "Well there's a surprise. What was the excuse?" I asked. "They are waiting for a delivery." she said. "Look I think you have been sold your own units twice, this situation needs to be brought to an end. Do you want me to speak with Geovox?" "See what you can do." she asked.

I contacted Mark White in Houston and outlined the problem; he contacted Immigration by return and immediately investigated the allegations. Mark White is a former attorney and, as I mentioned, past Governor of Texas, a good friend of the Clintons. Diplomacy came second nature. Piss him off and the mood changed, as you would expect. Not that I did, but I witnessed an incident in a restaurant when the owner tried to pull a fast one over the bill. That guy learnt a sharp lesson in front of a packed restaurant which fell silent as everyone witnessed an expert delivery of a complaint dealing with a 40% overcharge. Mark called me back as soon as he had been briefed and had the chance to speak to ISL.

"Barry, what do they (Immigration) want? How can we best deal with this matter?" "Mark, I'll e-mail you; I have a list of facts and figures, some of which I'm sure you can confirm or deny without any difficulty." I passed on the list of points that had been detailed to me. One item detailed a system that had had its plasma touch-screen damaged, necessitating a complete replacement screen. The invoice for the repair was twenty thousand pounds. Which had been paid. I knew that the most the repair should cost might be two thousand pounds. The problem was not just one item; the list went on and on. Ripped off, did not adequately describe the scenario!

Prolonged and shared incompetence in management of the procurement of the HBD systems hit me between the eyes.

I met with Mark White; he wanted me on board and offered me a contract with the direct responsibility for the EU with the exception of Italy, Spain and Turkey. He knew that I had many contacts in the Immigration service. Obviously he was looking at self-preservation of Geovox. Mark responded he terminated the ISL contract without further delay. Damage limitation was the order of the day. Having been at arms length (some 5,000 miles away) from the front line, this was to be his defence. Mark was not short on promises to put things right though and he tried.

Alas, the fiasco did not end there. I discovered a huge amount of money had been invested by Immigration in the establishment of search facilities at ports in France and Belgium, buildings costing two hundred and fifty thousand pounds a time. They had all been built in the wrong locations. The HBD systems did not function, environmental variations were causing chaos. Each building proudly displayed a large notice over the doors "Heart Beat Detection provided by HM Immigration".

The sign was one hell of a deterrent. The doors of the buildings were firmly locked.

Effactually they had erected these buildings costing £250,000 a time while assuming the HBD systems would just plug in and work. I can only guess someone sitting in an office at Croydon had signed off on this brain-wave.

"Oh what a mess." had been the comment that I'd noted at my meeting at Heathrow. Oh what an understatement. Each new probe with yet more incompetence revealed, and at what cost.

My estimate, which I suggest is pretty close to target, is that £10,000,000 yes ten million pounds was spent on this project. Only five percent, yes 5%, of the project has worked to anything like acceptable levels. A store-room in Dover contains a huge amount of, as yet, unused systems. How do I know? I collected one system from that very store. I saw the equipment with my own eyes.

The sixty thousand pounds was never repaid, I know that for a fact. The unit accounts were manipulated for six months, showing continued maintenance being provided for the HBD systems without any payment being made. This then balanced the books for any internal audit. A cover-up, no less.

Two immigration units, one DETMU located at Status Park, and the other at Dover, were involved. The Dover unit was directly responsible for operational logistics at all of the locations. Empire rivalry reared its ugly head. Inter-unit co-operation was a major hurdle to overcome. Old clashes were never forgiven; instead, revenge was taken at every provided opportunity. It was almost school playground level childish resentment.

During 2004 I visited all of the EU accession states whilst demonstrating the HMD. This provided a first class opportunity to obtain a front line knowledge of our prospective EU partners in waiting. Slovenia, Serbia, Croatia, Poland, Bulgaria, Turkey and Greece all wanted the equipment, provided it was paid for by the EU or UK.

Whilst I was in Bulgaria, I secured one order for a system. I returned a month later to install the system and to erect a building in which the unit was to be operated.

The location was on the Bulgarian / Turkish border. I knew the commander of the border police we had met previously. Fortunately I had an interpreter, which worked out fine. The construction took a full day to complete. At, mid day, the commander invited me to lunch with him and his deputy. We sat in an alfresco location. I was facing the entrance; the two Bulgarians had their backs to the entrance and were facing me. We communicated after a fashion. I noticed a black Mercedes pull up and two heavies get out. They both came into the restaurant and came straight over to our table. One of the guys put his hand on the commander's shoulder, whilst removing an envelope from his inside pocket of his black leather jacket. He spoke to the commander who flushed and clearly said "Not now, not now, fuck off." This would be the mafia paying their dues. It was so obvious; I didn't need to speak Bulgarian. Wages are so low, corruption is rife. As the EU borders extend, new criminal activities will head our way. The next ten years are going to be an era very different from any previous we have record. It will not be all pleasant experiences either; we are going to learn the hard way. Serious mistakes have been made which cannot be put right now; it just doesn't work that way.

Yet another procurement unit located in Croydon managed the contracts and here we may have the root of the problem. The unit was managed by a consultant, one of four consultants whom I encountered. These consultants were brought in on long term contracts to advise on procurement contracts. The fees are astronomical.

What an indictment. Here was a clear admission that the Home Office hierarchy was not capable of functioning without consultants to advise them. Obviously, when spending public money, the correct decisions must be made and accountability is essential. This I fully accept as being correct and proper. I have absolutely no argument with that position.

Advice on market products available and suitability for purpose is one thing but full time, long-term, resident consultants retained at extortionate fees does not represent savings in any shape or form.

We encountered two of the consultants: one a lady who, when accompanied by a female CIO, decided she would justify her existence. She did not know me from Adam but just assumed that I made a good target. We were on site at one of the search buildings where environmental conditions were difficult. This consultant threw a wobbler; she ranted and raved at me for nearly ten minutes. When she ran out of wind, I congratulated her on her stamina, adding that if only she had known what she was talking about, it might even have been constructive. If the building location had been selected correctly, this problem would not have been an issue. The consultant had not even considered that fact. I had just been asked to gather the data from this location.

I had spent four hours gathering data which was specific to this location. The HBD system as I mentioned earlier had a great track record in protected environments. The difficulties now were wind and vibration which, together, were by no means insignificant. The prevailing conditions were making the system ineffective for its task. When you consider another twelve systems were sitting in a store at Dover unused (£24,000) each unit £280,000 in total. Having gathered the data, I sent it back to Houston where it would be analysed and new algorithms would be integrated into the software in order to adjust and compensate for local conditions. That was the theory anyway; as we visited each site every location had marked local variations. The result indicated new software for each location would be the only way to eliminate the problem.

The HBD system is a self-teaching programme, so it needs to be given the stated parameters for each location; false readings are not productive and have to be eliminated.

I worked for long periods gathering data from all the locations with Colin Frazier, the sales director from Houston. The original systems were just sitting, gathering dust in the buildings erected for the task. Twenty thousand pounds (£24,000) a time, left idle and unattended. Not fit for purpose?

This situation was no different at all to that we had met in Calais the locations all had the same basic problem wind and vibration. In fact the new situation was exactly like that which we had encountered back in 2001, four years earlier. Did we not learn the lessons then? Obviously not.

The consultants wanted to blame the system, maybe that's what they thought the Home Office wanted to hear, no doubt. Did the consultants not think it prudent to seek advice from the system manufactures on the site locations for the examination buildings? No, that would be too simple. Let's erect two million pounds worth of buildings. They will look great.

In fact, I was told the plan was to build forty of these buildings. Good luck, I trust you'll put them in the right place. It would help.

A Mark11 version of the HBD software was produced, incorporating the data that had been collected from all of the problem locations and DETMU wanted five days of trials, which seemed a very good idea. I was asked to attend and assist for the duration of the tests.

Day one and the system worked well through- out the day at 95% accuracy, which was a vast improvement. Second day a new location, accuracy dipped to 85%. We did find two Indians concealed in a customs-sealed unit, which was proof that the system was functioning but this second location still needed work. The third day was a disaster: all the stored data was wiped from the system under directions from Houston the previous evening. We had to start from scratch; thirty hours of data had been erased. We had three hours to replace it, an impossible task. Our effort did not reflect success in the accuracy of the system, it nose dived to 64%.

Day four, yet another new location, and still a struggle but at least it was an improvement. Day five, yet another location and the tests there were completed by lunch time when we all left. The reason I mention these tests is because we were furnished with a copy of the test-results by Immigration. The days and locations were mixed up. Someone, I guessed, had dropped the papers on the floor or something of that nature; they did not tally with our records. This screwed up the specific data for each location which had been the primary objective of the task. Eight people had been involved in this five-day exercise and they still couldn't get the results lined up with the right day and the correct location. The farce continued.

The maintenance and support role, for which I had been contracted, was withdrawn. I was viewed as an ongoing problem. I knew far too much and I needed to be removed. The Home Office did not want me involved; they wanted to deal directly and only with Geovox in Houston. To fulfil a maintenance and service contract with sixteen locations in Europe from Houston in Texas is a tall order, to say the least.

All of the Home Office interference is added to the fact that I had a very frank exchange of e-mails with Andrew White, the new President of Geovox, outlining what I had seen as the true value of HBD and the half-cocked effort to upgrade the system. I had secured evidence that the upgrade to the HBD system had not been completed as Geovox were suggesting. Far from it, the Mark 11 system in its upgraded status only functioned to 75% of its capability. Geovox were demanding £9000 to upgrade each of the original Mark 1 systems. The upgrade process was additional software a task that took eleven minutes to upload.

I was not going to be a party to any contrary claim which I knew full well was rubbish. So, yet again, I was used while it suited them, and while they needed to extract themselves from the mire.

My last conversation with Andrew White was graphic and rather rude; it came as no surprise when I was dropped from the team. Let's just watch this space for the name of the former HM Immigration Director when he joins Geovox.

"BEST VALUE" MINISTER?

All of my involvement with deportation revolved around crime of some description. Most cases were serious offences and thus exceptionally risky individuals. These represented a small proportion of the overall total numbers coming into the UK.

The majority of illegals arriving are individuals seeking a better life in what they consider to be the Land of Opportunity. Whilst we don't want the criminal element, we should acknowledge the tenacity shown by those people. When you experience at first hand what they want to leave, it's not difficult to work out why. Thus the determination is the uppermost priority to reach their promised destination at all costs.

Risks to life and limb are ignored in utter desperation. Countless individuals pay the ultimate price in their attempts to reach the UK.

With the large numbers coming into the UK the chances of past criminal history coming to notice is next to zero. Recidivist offenders will come to notice and, with luck, be arrested. A Kenyan national that we were set up to remove comes to mind. The removal was cancelled due to yet another last minute appeal (about the third such appeal). A regular tactic. The subject was given bail.

Within forty-eight hours, he committed three rapes: two on women, and one on a sixteen- year old male on a train. The system let those three victims down in such a tragic way. Scarred for life, and there are many more who have been affected in such a way.

Yet another was a Tunisian paedophile. Five children suffered serious assaults at his hands.

Tunisian Airways refused to carry us. Not a peep from Immigration. The powers to ensure the removal were not invoked. I made sure it was British Airways the next time. He went.

Should we not be doing more to encourage the potential economic illegal migrant to build and develop their home lands? Not by throwing money at these countries, for it to be sorted away by corrupt regimes into Swiss bank accounts, but by providing material benefits so that they can work and receive payment for their effort? Emulating schemes that already exist here in the UK would be a good start.

I have tried to describe how we functioned over an eighteen-year period so that it is a matter of record. By identifying problem areas that have existed, comparisons can be drawn with the current situation. Has progress been made? Far from it, my regular frontline updates indicate progress is thin on the ground; in fact, chaos' is the constant description. Sixty percent of planned removals are cancelled prior to departure. All such non-events have a cost factor that is incurred.

Escorts are retained on a twelve thousand pound (£12,000) a year retainer whether they work or not. They are expected to respond when called upon. Operational difficulties are endless. No doubt this turmoil creates a false impression of value for money.

Health and Safety requirements have gone right out of the window. Progress? You must be kidding.

Flights are booked on the basis of the cheapest tickets available which makes sense and is understandable. Straight-turn-a-rounds are the order of the day. I find this rather difficult to understand for one very good reason. When I argued for either night-stops or

More leg-room for return flights of seven hours duration or longer, it was accepted as being in line with acknowledged health and safety requirements. The senior immigration officers who accepted this status are now running the enforcement department and have seen fit to revoke their own earlier decision. The health and safety of escorts is no longer a considered factor.

Control and Restraints have always been a bone of contention and still remains so. The elimination of the use of anti-bite gloves makes no sense whatsoever. Staff injuries sustained as the result of bites continues to increase, some of which have been very serious.

Securicor, having amalgamated with Group 4, now have the removal contract. Six years ago neither company wanted the contract. The fact that within the stated tender requirements neither company qualified by meeting the set criteria may well have been a factor. I am only able to refer to tender-requirements for 1997 and 2000 tendering procedures which may well have been changed since that time. Having made that point, the criterion I refer to is primary qualification. Any company taking part in the tendering process had to have a proven track record in deportation, before getting on the list of tendering companies.

The Home Office wouldn't move the primary criteria, would they? Any questions asked in this direction will be met with the bog standard reply. The phrase "Commercial in Confidence" confidentiality. Thus the cover-up is completed. It's the easy side step.

Operation Aardvark deals with the group removals. These are the people who willingly want to return to their country of origin. Aircraft are chartered and filled with subjects returning to one location. Sure: large numbers look good on the achieved total analysis. This makes sense and in most cases will prove to be cost effective. The hard line "High Risk" is not included in the figures for statistical purposes, and this is a whole different issue. Don't be misled by the spin over targets and achieved numbers. Clear manipulation of statistics takes place. The Home Office is not the only department to exploit such devious tactics.

The Belgium police tried the same operation by attempting to remove en-masse West African nationals, and the flight was abandoned due to a serious riot and extensive damage to the aircraft. The police were unable to control the situation to enable the flight to be concluded in safety.

The statistics of achieved completed removals would no doubt, make very interesting reading. To be combined with details of the cost ratio to successful completed removal. Are we getting value for money? After all, value for money was the key factor in the 1999 tender process. "Commercial Confidentiality" will be the answer to any questions asked of HM Immigration. It's the standard answer. Sorry, we haven't got a calculator, and why should we tell you anyway? Statistics that means keeping records? That just isn't going to happen. Historically, they play their cards close to their chests. Surely this information should be available, and the media need to demand the figures are provided and analysed.

No, more guesswork, is really not good enough. Just how many statistics issued by the IND have been accurate in the past ten years? Not one set of figures, they have all proved to be wrong subsequent, to delivery. What is the game being played out in the corridors of power?

My theory: I, along with many others, for years thought that corruption was endemic in third world countries. Having experienced corruption in various forms in the UK at first hand, I have detailed such events that I encountered.

The format which I am suggesting is by no means isolated or confined to just the Home Office. It is now part of the widely accepted fabric of our society. It is concentrated within the civil service. The NHS is a prime casualty of this utter dishonesty.

I refer to the deplorable practice of jobs for the boys. We have middle and senior management in all spheres of public service who, whilst employed, fail to discharge their duty in respect of policy-making or major decisions. The reason being they either can't do the job, or due to self protection elect not. They don't want to get it wrong and then jeopardise their reputation and position.

As retirement approaches they agree to take a commutation plus their pension. Two weeks later they appear back in the office with a new title, probably driving a new car, reinstated at their previous pay level. Having deposited the lump sum in the bank and have started to draw the index-linked pension.

Sound familiar? It's happening all the time. If the NHS budget is analysed closely, a substantial amount of money has been misused in this manner. Funds that should have produced direct benefit to patients or funded pay for nurses and lower paid staff have been redirected. Even funds which should purchase equipment or drugs have been redirected. I'm not referring to small change either: we are talking of millions of pounds if not billions.

How can these senior executives endorse the refusal of expensive vital, life-prolonging drugs on the basis of cost? Knowing full well that a large number of their colleagues have double dipped the funding. Are they avoiding the issue because their turn is rapidly approaching?

The alternative scenario, which is an open secret, is take your lump sum and pension but then come back as a consultant.

Having avoided making policy decisions whilst in the full-time post you can come back and advise us how to avoid the issue in the future. We will pay you an enhanced fee for the privilege. What is the fantastic transformation that takes place during the period between departure from post and re-emergence in secondary consultant placement?

Am I the only person that sees this corruption? Of course not, such incidents are witnessed continuously. The tragic factor is that the every-day witnesses need to earn a living, they have to pay their mortgages, they need to provide for their family, and keep their jobs, so they remain silent in fear of reprisals, if they should utter a word against the practices. Who can blame them?

Our infrastructure in this country is such that greed has taken control, from Government all the way down. It's now the accepted norm. No wonder the NHS is in crisis. The Home Office is in free fall, and all other departments follow the same format. It has to stop now. UK Ltd is haemorrhaging fast. This corruption, and I make no apology for using the term, is a blatant manipulation of the system. Genuine promotion and warranted advancement of worthy staff is stalled as a result of the manipulation I have described. This cannot be sustained: the gravy train needs to be derailed.

The Home Office immigration enforcement needs to be restructured and requires an injection of new blood. There is a wealth of young, keen, junior ranks that will, given the opportunity, reshape the department and make it "fit for purpose." I wish them well.

Well that's got a great deal off of my chest in a purely selfish way. I feel much better having aired my views between me and the computer. It becomes so totally exasperating when I read and hear so much waffle that occurs in the media these days: generated from half-truths and speculative rumours, often without foundation.

I feel almost embarrassed by the fact that my neighbours in our home town care desperately about this subject and want to make a clear independent judgement for themselves. They are prevented from doing so by misinformation or being completely hoodwinked by politicians and media hacks as to the true status of the situation in respect to immigration.

Clearly, very few people object to the acceptance of genuine asylum seekers. Where there is a justifiable major objection is in the influx of organised crime in the form of so called economic migrants. The laws are openly flouted in order to gain entry to rich pickings. Rich pickings for such anonymous people as the ones who recruit and employ Chinese cockle pickers...

This situation is by no means new or unique. It has existed for years. Our political leaders have just chosen to ignore the warning signs and all political parties share the blame. Having had ample opportunity to deal with the situation whilst in or out of power, but instead they have veered away.

The EU is easy pickings for criminals from Eastern Europe, for instance. The criminal fraternity cannot believe their luck and they will not miss the opportunity provided to them. We in the UK will encounter a major onslaught of criminal activities, the like of which we have experienced previously, but not yet anything like the volume to be expected. Our law enforcement agencies will struggle to cope with the onslaught. And they will fail to do more than slightly ease the damage and loss.

Criminal use of firearms will escalate along with the use of knives in the furtherance and completion of crimes. Are these also the acceptable factors within the equations? We are not told, of course, but are the direct questions ever asked in any shape or form? Do we settle for just commenting in passing when such crimes are described in news bulletins, or when we read the details in the press. Thus we are accepting these crimes as being inevitable and the norm that we can now expect.

Not so long ago we would quite often draw gloating comparisons with crime statistics in the USA against our own. These days in some aspects, we have overtaken the alarming figures and we are surging ahead of the States. Thirty years ago, we knew of the drugs culture and the anticipated epidemic that would develop. We are now one of the largest users of cocaine and heroin in the world. What an indictment!

Yardie reprisal shootings or stabbings, drug related crimes which now occur almost on a daily basis in this country have now become an accepted norm. Is this Progress? Or misguided acceptance of the inevitable? We just need to live with it and deal with the fringe offenders or addicts as a token gesture. Whilst claims are made that the situation is under control. A fool's paradise if ever there was one. Because we have not been directly involved does not mean it's not happening in our town. It is happening and right under our nose (no pun intended). Such crimes are a regular pattern of daily events of life and have been for years in Kingston Jamaica and many other hot spots throughout the world.

The UK is now one of the major drug centres of the world. Like it or not, this fact is a gigantic magnet for criminal enterprise. Is the MOD and our Government effectually presiding over the export of heroin from the vast poppy fields of Afghanistan? If so why? And who are reaping the profits?

Without controlled immigration there is no possible way checks can be instigated on every subject entering this country; the volume is just so vast. Neither, unless being previously informed, can the duty immigration officers be expected to identify the criminal element every time they arrive at the desk in Heathrow, Gatwick, Dover or Ashford. Information as to registered criminal history will not just pop up on the computer screens.

If the truth is known, a calculated risk is factored into the entry procedures. It's readily accepted that a certain percentage will of course overstay and vanish into the chasm of major conurbations. A further percentage will commit crimes of various levels of seriousness; the chances of the offenders being caught in the first instance are fairly remote. Organised petty criminal groups derive rich pickings and are rarely prosecuted.

I fail to understand what is wrong with publishing the full facts and figures on a quarterly basis. Surely, with the true situation disclosed, the adverse speculation and the misinformation are eliminated. Either the true situation is not known or yet another stronger motive dictates the manner in which statistics are published after having been totally manipulated.

Drastic changes need to be made in order to stabilise our immediate security and the economic future of our country. Of course we need immigrants within the scope of the economy: mutual benefits are derived from their efforts. Should we be cherry-picking the crème de la crème from countries that are in desperate need of a stable infrastructure of their own? Such countries are unable to sustain the loss of their own professional structure of expertise.

By allowing, and endorsing, the removal of these stratums of expertise whatever the level, we inflict further hardship on the country of origin, whether directly or indirectly.

Let's establish control of the situation and not promote the black economy which has been the result to date. Control must be regained from the sheer chaos of the last ten years; the mistakes must not be repeated. It might well be deemed unpalatable to some but control is essential.

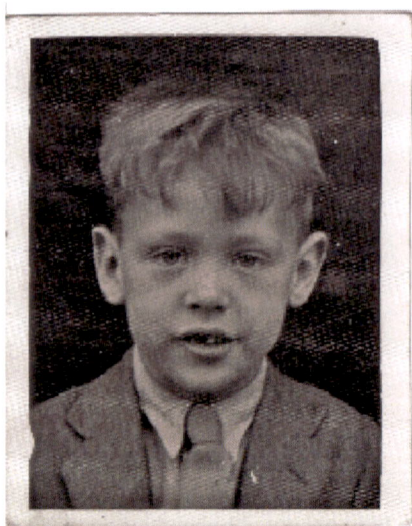

Undergoing astronaut training

Aged six

Embarking upon the voyage of life

City of Ely

1963 Barking to Southend M260

BAe 125 800 G-TSAM
Cessna Conquest Mk11 G-SOFE

Home, not as we know it

Wash day Abidjan

My first Office at The Beehive Gatwick

Lear 35 G-SOVN